The King and His Kingdom
in
ACTS

Lucian Farrar, Jr.

James Kay Publishing

Tulsa, Oklahoma

The King and His Kingdom in Acts
ISBN 978-1-943245-72-7

www.jameskaypublishing.com

e-mail: sales@jameskaypublishing.com

© 2022 Lucian Farrar, Jr.
Cover design by JKP
Author Photo by Bob Cooper

1.1
All rights reserved.
No part of this book may be reproduced in any form
or by any means
- except for review questions and brief quotations -
without permission in writing from the author.

These were Incorporated into the Cover

https://www.freecreatives.com/clipart/crown-clip-arts.html

ipcc_bluemarble_west_lrg.jpg (3718×3718) (nasa.gov)

Other Books by Lucian Farrar, Jr.

The Book of Daniel
The Most High Rules
A Commentary and Questions

The Victorious Church
In the Book of Revelation
A Commentary and Questions

The Minor Prophets
God's Spokesmen
A Commentary and Questions

The Book of Isaiah
Christ, Our Redeemer
A Commentary and Questions

The Life of Christ
A Chronological Account

Psalms
Book 1
David's Original Collection

Psalms
Books 2 & 3

The King James Version is used for the most part in this book. Some archaic words have been replaced. Whenever verbs are before the subject of a declarative sentence, the word order has been changed to avoid being misunderstood as a question. Present-day punctuations have been used.

Other translations are acknowledged
by the following abbreviations:
ASV – American Standard Version
ESV – English Standard Version
NASB – New American Standard Bible, 1973
NIV – New International Version, 1996
NKJV – New King James Version, 1996

These translations are used to replace archaic words with those that can be understood today or to give a more accurate meaning of the original text.

Dedication

This book is dedicated to my daughter,

Melisa Kay (Farrar) Jones.

Melisa's very first words were, "I love you." And her life has demonstrated her love. She has always wanted to do what is right. When she was two years old, she kept her two older brothers in line by pointing a finger at them and saying, "Don't!"

Melisa has a beautiful singing voice. As a four-year old, she would sing herself to sleep every night, making up words to the tune of "O How I Love Jesus." When she was in the eighth grade, she sang a solo in her school's music concert. She was in special singing groups during her high school years. I treasure recordings of her singing with her mother and later with her husband, Norman.

As a teenager, Melisa participated in Bible bowls, and she received the first-place trophy at Omaha, Nebraska for having the highest percentage of correct answers. After graduating from high school, she coached Bible bowl teams. She made a notebook of questions and answers for the entire book of Acts.

Melisa serves as a paralegal for Blue Cross & Blue Shield of Kansas. Her desire in life has been to follow the example of her Lord Jesus Christ, "who went about doing good." (Acts 10:38)

— Lucian Farrar, Jr.

Thank you,
> To Bob Colvin for proofreading this book.

Table of Contents

Dedication ix

The King and His Kingdom 1

Acts 1:1 – 2:21, The Kingdom Established 11

Acts 2:22-47, The King on His Throne 19

Acts 3:1 – 4:31, The King's Power to Save 27

Acts 4:32 – 5:42, The Apostles Are Witnesses 37

Acts 6:1 – 8:3, The First Christian Martyr 45

Acts 8:4-40, Philip the Evangelist 57

Acts 9:1-31, The Conversion of Saul 67

Acts 9:32 – 11:18, The Ministry of Peter 75

Acts 11:19 – 12:25, Power over Persecutors 85

Acts 13 – 14, The First Missionary Journey 93

Acts 15, The Meeting at Jerusalem 111

Acts 16, The Second Missionary Journey 119

Acts 17, Thessalonica to Athens 131

Acts 18, Corinth to Antioch 141

Acts 19, The Third Missionary Journey 151

Acts 20, The Conclusion of the Journey 161

Acts 21, The Journey to Jerusalem 171

Acts 22, Paul's Defense before a Mob 179

Acts 23, The Plot against Paul 187

Acts 24, Governor Felix Hears Paul 197

Acts 25, Paul Appeals to Caesar 205

Acts 26. King Agrippa Hears Paul 213

Acts 27, The Voyage to Rome 221

Acts 28, Paul at Rome 231

Bibliography 239

The King and His Kingdom

*"God has made that same Jesus,
whom you have crucified,
both Lord and Christ."*
Acts 2:36

"Jesus is Lord and Christ." This is the theme of Acts. A ***lord*** is a person of power. ***Christ*** means "anointed." The Book of Acts reveals the King and his Kingdom.

Peter proclaimed that Jesus is the Christ in Acts 2:22-36. The prophets had foretold the coming of the Messiah, the "Seed of Abraham," who would bless all the families of the earth. (Acts 3:25-26) Peter declared, "Neither is there salvation in any other: for there is none other name under heaven given among men whereby we must be saved." (Acts 4:12). "The God of our fathers raised up Jesus, whom you slew and hanged on a tree. God has exalted him with his right hand to be a Prince and a Savior." (Acts 5:30-31) The apostles "ceased not to teach and preach Jesus Christ." (Acts 5:42)

Philip the evangelist preached Christ in Samaria. (Acts 8:5) And he preached Jesus to the treasurer of the Queen of Ethiopia. (Acts 8:26-35) After his conversion, Saul of Tarsus immediately proclaimed Jesus in the synagogues, saying, "He is the Son of God." (Acts 9:20) Peter instructed Cornelius and his household that Jesus Christ is "Lord of all." (Acts 10:36)

In Pisidian Antioch during his first missionary journey, Paul revealed that God had raised up a Savior, Jesus. (Acts 13:23) In the closing chapter of Acts, we find Paul in Rome, "preaching the kingdom of God and teaching those things which concern the Lord Jesus Christ." (Acts 28:31)

Jesus is the Christ, **"the Anointed One,"** to be our **Prophet** (Acts 3:22-23), our **Priest** (Hebrews 4:15) and our **King** (Acts 2:29-35). Jesus Christ is now reigning over his kingdom. This kingdom of God is mentioned in Acts 1:3, Acts 8:12, Acts 14:22, Acts 19:8, Acts 20:25, Acts 28:23 and Acts 28:31.

During his ministry, Jesus preached the coming of the kingdom of God. (Luke 8:1) He said there were those in his audience that would not die until they had seen the kingdom of God having come with power. (Mark 9:1) Over a period of forty days after his resurrection, Jesus was "speaking of the things pertaining to the kingdom of God." (Acts 1:3) Before he ascended into heaven, Jesus promised his apostles that they would "be baptized with the Holy Spirit." (Acts 1:5) At that time, they would "receive power." (Acts 1:8) On the day of Pentecost the power came, and the kingdom was established. There was a sound from heaven as of a rushing mighty wind. And a crowd of people came together and saw "tongues like as of fire" upon the apostles, and they heard them speak in other languages as the Spirit was giving them the words. (Acts 2:1-12) "And the same day there were added unto them about three thousand souls." (Acts 2:41) "And the Lord added to the church daily such as should be saved." (Acts 2:47)

The book of Acts records the power of the Holy Spirit in the early church. Jesus had promised his apostles that the Father would send the Holy Spirit, who would teach them all things and bring to their remembrance all things that he had said to them. (John 14:26) The Holy Spirit would testify of Jesus, and also the apostles would bear witness. (John 15:26-27) They would be guided into all truth by the Spirit, who would reveal additional teachings of Christ to them. (John 16:12-14)

In Peter's sermon on the day of Pentecost, he quoted the prophecy of Joel, "I will pour out of my Spirit upon all flesh, and your sons and your daughters shall prophesy and your young men shall see visions and your old men shall dream dreams. And I will show wonders in heaven above and signs in the earth beneath." (Acts 2:17, 19) Peter concluded, "Therefore let all the house of Israel know assuredly that God has made that same Jesus, whom you have crucified, both Lord and Christ." When the people heard this, they asked, "What shall we do?" Peter said to them, "Repent and be baptized every one of you in the name of Jesus Christ for the remission of sins, and ye shall **receive the gift of the Holy Spirit**." (Acts 2:38) When and how did they **receive** the gift of the Holy Spirit?

Philip the evangelist went to the city of Samaria and preached Christ, and he worked various miracles to confirm his words. When they believed, they were baptized. (Acts 8:5-12) "Now when the apostles who were at Jerusalem heard that Samaria had received the word of God, they sent to them Peter and John ... that they might **receive the Holy Spirit.** (For as yet he was fallen upon none of them; only they were baptized in the name of the Lord Jesus.) Then they laid their hands on them, and they **received** the Holy Spirit." (Acts 8:14-17) Those that were baptized did not immediately receive the gift of the Holy Spirit. When apostles laid their hands on them, they received the gift of the Holy Spirit.

Another example is found in Acts 19:1-7. Paul came to Ephesus and found twelve disciples. He asked them, "Have you **received** the Holy Spirit since you believed?" They said they had not heard of the Holy Spirit, because they had been baptized with John's baptism. So, Paul baptized them in the name of the Lord Jesus. "And when Paul had laid his hands upon them, the Holy Spirit came on them; and they spoke with tongues and prophesied." Paul, an apostle, had to lay his hands on these baptized believers for them to **receive** the Holy Spirit. They "were sealed with the Holy Spirit" by miraculous gifts: speaking in other languages and prophesying. (Ephesians 1:13)

The conversion of Cornelius and his household proves that the gift of the Holy Spirit was a miraculous gift. "While Peter was still speaking these words, the Holy Spirit fell upon all those who heard the word. And those of the circumcision who believed were astonished, as many as came with Peter, because **the gift of the Holy Spirit had been poured out on the Gentiles also. For they heard them speak with tongues** and magnify God." NKJV The miraculous power given to Cornelius and his household convinced Peter and the Christians with him that these Gentiles should be baptized. (Acts 10:44-48) Let the Bible tell us what the gift is. The gift of the Holy Spirit was miraculous as Joel had predicted.

The apostles and the first Gentile converts were the only ones who received the baptism of the Holy Spirit. The miraculous power that came upon the apostles on Pentecost was the baptism of the Holy Spirit. (Acts 1:5, 1:26 – 2:4) When Peter reported on his preaching to the Gentiles, he said, "As I began to speak, the Holy Spirit fell on them as on us at the beginning. Then I remembered the word of the Lord, how he said, 'John indeed baptized with water; but you shall be baptized with the Holy Spirit.'" (Acts 11:15-16) The baptism of the Holy Spirit describes a **method**. It was a direct pouring out of the Spirit's power without a human agency—the laying on of hands. Cornelius and the apostles did **not** receive the same **measure** of the Spirit's power. The baptism of the Holy Spirit upon Gentiles was instructive: it convinced the apostles that "God has also to the Gentiles granted repentance unto life." (Acts 11:1, 18)

The Holy Spirit is not just a power; he is a person. Jesus Christ is a person. What is the gift of Christ? His mission was the eternal salvation of our souls! Jesus said in John 3:16, "For God so love the world that he gave his only begotten Son, that whosoever believes in him should not perish but have everlasting life." What then is the gift of the Holy Spirit? What was His mission?

The miraculous gifts of the Holy Spirit were for the purpose of revealing and confirming the gospel of Christ. Jesus explained the mission of the Holy Spirit to his apostles when he said, "The Holy Spirit, whom the Father will send in My name, He will teach you all things and bring to your remembrance all things that I have said to you." NKJV (John 14:26) Peter later wrote, "His divine power has given unto us all things that pertain unto life and godliness." (2 Peter 1:3) The Holy Spirit's mission has been accomplished. Hebrews 2:3-4 asks, "How shall we escape if we neglect so great salvation, which at the first began to be spoken by the Lord and **was confirmed** unto us by them that heard him; God also bearing them witness both with signs and wonders, and with various miracles and gifts of the Holy Spirit."

These miraculous gifts ceased with the passing of the apostles and with the completion of the Holy Bible, according to 1 Corinthians 13:8-10. If the Holy Spirit had not been sent, we would not have the books of the New Testament to read. We receive the gift of the Holy Spirit today when we study the New Testament and obey its teachings. We have the Spirit when we have His word abiding in us. (Romans 8:5) The Holy Spirit's words are Christ's words. (John 16:12-16) Jesus said, "It is the Spirit who gives life. The words that I speak to you are spirit, and they are life." (John 6:63) "If you abide in My word, you are My disciples indeed." NKJV (John 8:31)

Acts reveals that Jesus Christ fulfilled **"the promise"** that God made to the fathers: Abraham, Isaac and Jacob. The LORD said to Abraham, "In your seed shall all the nations of the earth be blessed." (Genesis 22:18) This promise was repeated to his son Isaac and to his grandson Jacob. (Genesis 26:4 and 28:14) In Galatians 3:16, Paul states that Christ is the promised Seed. This promise is the theme of the Bible, from Genesis to Revelation. (Read Revelation 5:9, 7:9 and 21:24-27.)

In Peter's sermon on Pentecost, he instructed believers to repent and be baptized in the name of Jesus Christ for the remission of sins; and then he said, "For **the promise** is to you and your children (the Jews) and to all that are afar off (the Gentiles), even as many as the Lord our God shall call." (Acts 2:39) In Peter's second recorded sermon, Peter mentioned "the covenant which God made with our fathers, saying to Abraham, 'And in your seed shall all the families of the earth be blessed.' Unto you first God, having raised up his Son Jesus, **sent him to bless you, in turning away every one of you from his iniquities**." (Acts 3:25-26) The nature of the blessing is spiritual: the forgiveness of sins.

At Antioch in Pisidia, Paul said, "According to **promise**, God has brought to Israel a Savior, Jesus. And we preach to you the good news of **the promise** made to the fathers, that God has fulfilled this promise to our children in that He raised up Jesus. Therefore, let it be known to you, brethren, that through Him forgiveness of sins is proclaimed to you." ^NASB (Acts 13:23, 32-33, 38)

Paul used this promise as his defense before King Agrippa. He said, "And now I stand and am judged for the hope of **the promise** made of God to our fathers. For which hope's sake, King Agrippa, I am accused of the Jews." (Acts 26:6-7) The Jews were accusing Paul for extending God's blessings to the Gentiles, and Paul uses the promise made to the fathers to show that the blessing included the Gentiles, when God said, "In your Seed shall all the nations of the earth be blessed." (Genesis 22:18)

The greatest blessing of all is the forgiveness of sins, made possible by the death, burial, and resurrection of Jesus Christ. The book of Acts gives examples of how sinners were forgiven and became servants of Christ in his kingdom.

On the day of Pentecost, Peter preached the gospel of Christ, being inspired by the Holy Spirit. (Acts 2:4, 14-36). Those who were convinced that Jesus is now Lord and Christ, asked, "What shall we do?" (Acts 2:37) Peter answered, "Repent, and let each one of you be baptized in the name of Jesus Christ for the forgiveness of your sins." NASB (Acts 2:38) "Then they that gladly received the word were baptized, and the same day there were added to them about three thousand souls." (Acts 2:41)

Philip the evangelist went down to the city of Samaria and preached Christ to them. (Acts 8:5) "When they believed Philip preaching the kingdom of God and the name of Jesus Christ, they were baptized." (Acts 8:12) Jesus said, "He that believes and is baptized shall be saved." (Mark 16:16)

Philip also preached Jesus to the Ethiopian eunuch, who was on the road to Gaza. (Acts 8:26-35) When they came to some water, the Ethiopian asked, "What hinders me to be baptized?" And Philip said, "If you believe with all your heart, you may." And they both went down into the water, and Philip baptized him. (Acts 8:37-38)

On the road to Damascus, Jesus appeared to Saul of Tarsus, who would be known later as the apostle Paul. When Saul asked, "What will you have me to do?" The Lord told him, "Arise, and go into the city, and it shall be told you what you must do." Saul, who had been blinded by a great light, was led into the city of Damascus; and he fasted and prayed for three days. The Lord sent a disciple named Ananias to restore Paul's sight and tell him what to do. In his own words, Paul says that Ananias told him,

"Arise and be baptized and wash away your sins, calling on the name of the Lord." (Acts 22:12-16)

An angel answered the prayers of Cornelius and instructed him to send for Peter, who would tell him and his family words of salvation. (Acts 11:13-14) Peter came and told Cornelius and his household that through the name of Jesus "whoever believes in him shall receive the remission of sins." Then Peter "commanded them to be baptized in the name of the Lord." (Acts 10:38-43, 48)

When Lydia "heard" the gospel, "she was baptized." (Acts 16:14-15) "Faith comes by hearing, and hearing by the word of God." (Romans 10:17)

The Philippian jailer was told to "believe on the Lord Jesus Christ," and then Paul and Silas "spoke the word of the Lord to him and to all who were in his house" so they could believe. The jailor then "took them the same hour of the night and washed their stripes. Immediately he and all of his family were baptized." NKJV (Acts 16:31-33)

"And many of the Corinthians, hearing, believed and were baptized." (Acts 18:8) The blessing of salvation from sins begins with hearing the gospel of Christ, which produces faith, and is completed in baptism. This is seen in all the examples of conversion in the book of Acts.

Acts is primarily about two apostles, Peter and Paul, covering a period of twenty-nine years. The first twelve chapters are mainly about Peter, and the last sixteen chapters cover Paul's missionary journeys and his trip to Rome for his first trial before Caesar in AD 62. The book was probably written soon after Paul was released from his first imprisonment. (Acts 28:30)

The purpose of Acts is to show what Jesus continued to do and teach through his body, the church, empowered by the Holy Spirit.

David Roper sees the Holy Spirit in Luke's writings: "Luke's inspiration was probably the results of the laying on of hands by Paul. It was Paul's practice to lay his hands on Christians to give them miraculous abilities (Acts 19:6; Rom. 1:11). Paul laid his hands on another of his traveling companions (2 Timothy 1:6); it is unlikely that he would not have laid his hands on Luke. Prophecy would have been an obvious gift for Luke to receive." [1]

Jesus instructed his apostles, "You shall be witnesses unto me both in Jerusalem and Judea, and in Samaria, and unto the uttermost part of the earth." (Acts 1:8) Their witness in Jerusalem is reported in Acts 1 – 7; their witness in Judea and Samaria is recorded in Acts 8 – 12; and their witness to the uttermost part of the earth is seen in Acts 13 – 28. They took the gospel of Christ from the city of Jerusalem to Rome, the ruling city of the world.

Sir William Ramsey, an archaeologist, retraced Paul's journeys in Asia in order to prove the then fashionable theory that Acts was the product of the second century. Gradually he was compelled to reverse his views by the evidence of facts he uncovered. He concluded, "Luke is a historian of the first rank."

F. F. Bruce observes, "The historical trust-worthiness of Luke has indeed been acknowledged by many biblical critics." [2]

---

[1] David Roper, *Truth for Today Commentary—Acts 1-14*, p. 6
[2] F. F. Bruce, *The New Testament Documents*, pp. 90-91

NOTES

The Kingdom Is Established
Acts 1:1 – 2:21

The former treatise I have made, O Theophilus, of all that Jesus began both to do and teach, until the day in which he was taken up, after that he through the Holy Spirit had given commands to the apostles whom he had chosen. 1:1-2

The Gospel According to Luke was previously written to "most excellent Theophilus." (Luke 1:3) So, Luke is also the writer of Acts. "Most excellent" is "the normal title for a high official in the Roman government." [3] Theophilus was a common name, and it means "friend of God." [4] Although the book was written to an individual reader, its message is for all who would be a friend of God. Luke's account of the gospel shows what Jesus began to do and teach, until the day he was taken up. (Luke 24:50-51) And the book of Acts reports what Jesus continues to do and teach through the church, his kingdom. The apostles of Christ were carrying out his commands through the Holy Spirit.

To whom also he showed himself alive after his passion by many infallible proofs, being seen of them for forty days, and speaking of the things pertaining to the kingdom of God. 1:3

Luke gave undeniable proofs of the resurrection of Jesus in Luke 24:1-43. Jesus appeared to his disciples during a period of forty days. He invited them to touch him, and he ate food with them. Jesus was preparing his disciples for the kingdom of God that would soon be established.

---

[3] William Barclay, *The Gospel of Luke,* p. xiii
[4] Anthony Lee Ash, *The Gospel According to Luke, Part I,* p. 23

"And being assembled together with *them*, He commanded them not depart from Jerusalem, but to wait for the Promise of the Father, "which," *He said*, "you have heard from Me; for John truly baptized with water, but you shall be baptized with the Holy Spirit not many days from now." NKJV **1:4-5**

The apostles were not to leave Jerusalem. (Luke 24:49) The promise of the Father was the one that the apostles had heard from Jesus. Jesus promised that the Father would send the Holy Spirit who would teach them all things. (John 14:26)

Therefore, when they had come together, they asked Him saying, "Lord, will You at this time restore again the kingdom to Israel?" NKJV **1:6** His apostles were looking for a great earthly kingdom like that of David and Solomon.

And he said to them, "It is not for you to know the times or the seasons which the Father has put in his own power. But you shall receive power, after that the Holy Spirit has come upon you. And you shall be witnesses to me both in Jerusalem, and in all Judea, and unto the uttermost part of the earth." 1:8

Jesus had said the kingdom of God would come with power. (Mark 9:1) The apostles would know that the kingdom had come when they received power from the Holy Spirit. Jesus instructed them saying, "Repentance and remission of sins should be preached in his name among all nations, beginning at Jerusalem." And he added, "And you are witnesses." (Luke 24:47-48) Jesus had said, "The Spirit of truth, who proceeds from the Father, he shall testify of me; and you also shall bear witness of me." (John 15:26-27) The Holy Spirit would bear witness of Jesus through the apostles, inspiring them and confirming their message with signs.

The Kingdom Is Established | 13

And when he had spoken these things, while they beheld, he was taken up; and a cloud received him out of their sight." 1:9

In a prophetic vision, the prophet Daniel had seen the Christ, the Son of Man, coming through the clouds of heaven to the Father, the Ancient of Days, and receiving glory and a kingdom. And "his kingdom is the one which shall not be destroyed." NKJV (Daniel 7:13-14)

And while they looked steadfastly toward heaven as he went up, behold, two men stood by them in white apparel, who also said, "Ye men of Galilee, why stand ye gazing up into heaven? This same Jesus, who is taken up from you into heaven, shall so come in like manner as ye have seen him go into heaven." 1:10-11

As the apostles watched Jesus as he ascended into heaven, two angels appeared to them as men dressed in white. They promised that Jesus would return again. "Behold, he comes with clouds, and every eye shall see him, and they also who pierced him." (Revelation 1:7)

Then they returned to Jerusalem from the mount called Olivet, which is from Jerusalem a sabbath day's journey. And when they were come in, they went up into an upper room, where abode Peter and James and John and Andrew, Philip and Thomas, Bartholomew and Matthew, James the son of Alphaeus and Simon the Zealot and Judas the son of James. These all continued with one accord in prayer and supplication with the women, and Mary the mother of Jesus, and with his brethren. 1:13-14

The apostles and other disciples were waiting for the coming of the kingdom by praying together. The women may have included Mary and Martha (Luke 10:38), and the women who had ministered to the needs of Jesus and his disciples (Luke 8:2-3). Mary the mother of Jesus and his brothers were also there. During his ministry, Jesus' brothers did not believe in him, according to John 7:5. After his resurrection, Jesus appeared to his oldest brother James. (1 Cor. 15:7) James likely shared the good news with his brothers: Joseph, Simon and Jude (Matt. 13:55), because they all became believers. The apostles were continually in the temple. (Luke 24:53) And altogether there were about a hundred and twenty disciples meeting with them in anticipation of the coming kingdom. **1:15**

And in those days Peter stood up in the midst of the disciples and said, "Men and brethren, this Scripture must needs have been fulfilled, which the Holy Spirit by the mouth of David spoke before concerning Judas, who was guide to them who took Jesus. For he was numbered with us and obtained a part in this ministry." 1:15-17

David's associate, Ahithophel, had joined Absalom's conspiracy against David. This betrayal of David by Ahithophel is used to typically predict the betrayal of Jesus by Judas: *"Yes, my own familiar friend in whom I trusted, who did eat my bread, has lifted up his heel against me."* Psalm 41:9

(Now this man purchased a field with the wages of iniquity; and falling headlong, he burst open in the middle and all his entrails gushed out. And it became known to all those dwelling in Jerusalem; so that field is called in their own language, Akel Dama, that is Field of Blood.) NKJV **1:18-19**

Luke describes the death of Judas. Matthew gives us more details of what Judas did. Judas confessed that he had sinned by betraying innocent blood, and he threw down the pieces of silver in the temple. He then departed and hanged himself. This blood money was used by the chief priests to buy a potter's field to bury strangers. (Matthew 27:4-5) After hanging himself, the rope or the branch broke, and the decomposing body of Judas fell bursting upon the rocks below. After interpreting the Aramaic words for Field of Blood in verse 19, Luke continues with Peter's words in verse 20.

"For it is written in the book of Psalms: 'Let his dwelling be desolate, and let no one live in it,' and 'Let another take his office.' Therefore, of these men who have accompanied us all the time that the Lord Jesus went in and out among us, beginning from the baptism of John to that day when He was taken up from us, one of these must become a witness with us of His resurrection." NKJV **1:20-22**

Peter refers to Psalm 69:25 and Psalm 109:8. The word *bishopric* in the King James Version refers to the office of an overseer. During the forty days following his resurrection, Jesus may have instructed the apostles to fill the vacancy left by Judas' death, giving the necessary qualifications.

And they appointed two: Joseph called Barsabas, who was surnamed Justus, and Matthias. And they prayed and said, "Thou, Lord, who knows the hearts of men, show which of these two thou hast chosen, that he may take part in this ministry and apostleship from which Judas by transgression fell, that he might go to his own place." And they gave forth their lots; and the lot fell upon Matthias, and he was numbered with the eleven apostles. 1:23-26

Now there were twelve apostles.

And when the day of Pentecost was fully come, they were all with one accord in one place. And suddenly there

came a sound from heaven as of a rushing mighty wind, and it filled the house where they were sitting. And there appeared to them cloven tongues like as of fire, and it sat upon each of them. And they were all filled with the Holy Spirit and began to speak as the Spirit gave them utterance. 2:1-4

On this day of Pentecost following the crucifixion of Jesus, the promise made to the fathers and the prophecies of the kingdom were being fulfilled. The kingdom of God was established with power. There was a sound of a violent wind. There appeared tongues of fire that divided and were distributed upon each of the apostles, and the apostles were able to speak in other languages as the Spirit gave them the words. This was the baptism of the Holy Spirit that Jesus had promised his apostles. (1:5)

And there were dwelling at Jerusalem Jews, devout men, out of every nation under heaven. 2:5

Isaiah the prophet had predicted, "And it shall come to pass in the last days, that the mountain of the LORD's house shall be established ... and all nations shall flow unto it. For out of Zion shall go forth the law, and the word of the LORD from Jerusalem." (Isaiah 2:2-3) The word "mountain" is a symbol for "kingdom." God's house is the church of the living God. (1 Timothy 3:15) The kingdom of God's church would be established in Jerusalem, and those of all nations would come into it.

When they heard this sound, a crowd came together in bewilderment, because each one heard them speaking in his own language. Utterly amazed, they asked: "Are not all these men who are speaking Galileans? Then how is it that each of us hears them in his own native language?" NIV **2:6-8**

Upon hearing the sound of a mighty wind, a great crowd gathered at the source of the sound. The apostles were in the temple, according to Luke 24:53. Those from the nations named in **2:9-11** wanted to know what all this meant. **2:12** However, there were some in the crowd who did not understand any of these foreign languages. They thought the apostles were drunk with new wine. **2:13**

But Peter, standing up with the eleven, lifted up his voice and said to them, "Ye men of Judea and all ye that dwell at Jerusalem, be this known to you and listen to my words. For these are not drunken, as ye suppose, seeing it is but the third hour of the day." 2:14

Peter was standing up with eleven other men – the apostles. When the church was established on the day of Pentecost, only the apostles were baptized with the Holy Spirit. The third hour of their day would be our nine o'clock in the morning. The apostles were not drunk. They were receiving miraculous power from the Holy Spirit as promised in Joel 2:28-32. Peter explained:

"But this is that which was spoken by the prophet Joel: 'And it shall come to pass in the last days, says God, I will pour out of my Spirit upon all flesh, and your sons and your daughters shall prophesy and your young men shall see visions, and your old men shall dream dreams. And on my servants and on my handmaidens, I will pour out of my Spirit; and they shall prophesy. And I will show wonders in heaven above and signs in the earth beneath, blood and fire, and vapor of smoke, before that great and notable day of the Lord come. And it shall come to pass, that whosoever shall call upon the name of the Lord shall be saved.'" 2:16-21

The Holy Spirit's gift would be poured out upon those of all nations. Men and women were given miraculous gifts of the Holy Spirit when the apostles laid their hands on them. (Acts 8:16-17) The scenes depicted in verses 19 and 20 describe the events when Jesus was crucified. The sun was darkened at noon. There was "blood, fire, and vapor of smoke" when the Passover lambs were sacrificed. When Jesus died, the veil of the temple was torn in two from top to bottom. The earth quaked, and rocks were split, and graves were opened. (Matthew 27:51-52) These signs came **before that great day** of the Lord – the day of Pentecost when the kingdom of God was established.

Joel concluded his prophecy with a promise: **And it shall come to pass, that whosoever shall call upon the name of the Lord shall be saved.**

Calling upon the name of the Lord is more than saying a prayer. Jesus had said, "Not everyone that says to me, 'Lord, Lord,' shall enter into the kingdom of heaven, but he that does the will of my Father who is in heaven." (Matt. 7:21) Paul also quotes the prophecy of Joel 2:32 in Romans 10:13. However, Paul tells us how he called on the name of the Lord for salvation in Acts 22:16. He was instructed, "Arise and be baptized and wash away your sins, calling on the name of the Lord." At the conclusion of his sermon, Peter told believers what they must do to be saved in verse 38. He did not tell them to repeat the sinner's prayer.

The King on His Throne
Acts 2:22-47

"Ye men of Israel, hear these words: Jesus of Nazareth, a man approved of God among you by miracles and wonders and signs which God did by him in the midst of you, as you yourselves also know— Him, being delivered by the determined counsel and foreknowledge of God, ye have taken and by wicked hands have crucified and slain, whom God has raised up." 2:22-24

Jesus proved that he was from God by the miracles he performed. He healed all kinds of diseases, made the lame to walk, the blind to see and the deaf to hear. He cast demons out of those being tormented in various ways. He multiplied loaves and fish to feed five thousand. He calmed the storms. He even raised the dead. Nicodemus, a ruler of the Jews, said to him, "No man can do these miracles that you do, except God is with him." (John 3:2)

Peter declared the gospel of Christ – His death, burial, and resurrection. (1 Corinthians 15:1-4) His death was no accident. He did not die as a victim of the Jewish leaders. His death was the atoning sacrifice for our sins, according to God's purpose and foreknowledge. He came into the world to die for us. (Matthew 20:28) John the Baptist introduced Jesus as "The Lamb of God who takes away the sin of the world." (John 1:29)

"For David says concerning Him: 'I foresaw the LORD** always before my face, for He is at my right hand, that I may not be shaken. Therefore, my heart rejoiced, and my tongue was made glad; moreover, my flesh also will rest in hope, for You will not leave my soul in Hades, nor will You allow Your Holy One to see corruption. You have**

made known to me the ways of life; You will make me full of joy in Your presence.'

"Men and brethren, let me speak freely to you of the patriarch David, that he is both dead and buried, and his tomb is with us to this day. Therefore, being a prophet, and knowing that God had sworn with an oath to him that of the fruit of his body, according to the flesh, He would raise up the Christ to sit on his throne, he, foreseeing this, spoke concerning the resurrection of the Christ, that His soul was not left in Hades, nor did His flesh see corruption." NKJV **2:25-31**

Peter quoted Psalm 16:8-11 by David showing that the resurrection of the Christ was predicted by God. David was not speaking about himself, because he was dead and his flesh saw corruption. But David, being a prophet, spoke of the resurrection of the Christ to sit on his throne.

"This Jesus God has raised up, whereof we all are witnesses." 2:32

David Roper suggests, "When he said, **we all**, he probably waved his arm, indicating the other eleven. The Old Testament said that 'on the evidence of two or three witnesses a matter shall be confirmed' (Deut. 19:15). Peter's audience was looking not at two or three **witnesses**, but at twelve men of unimpeachable character who personally had nothing to gain—and everything to lose—by preaching Christ. Ultimately, all but one of the men standing before Peter's listeners would be killed for his faith." [5] After the coming of the Holy Spirit's power upon the apostles, we can see a significant difference in them. They now understood the spiritual nature of the kingdom of God. Hear what Peter says next!

---

[5] David L. Roper, *Truth for Today Commentary, Acts 1-14*, p. 76

"Therefore, being by the right hand of God exalted and having received of the Father the promise of the Holy Spirit, he has shed forth this which ye now see and hear. For David is not ascended into the heavens, but he said himself, 'The LORD said to my Lord, "Sit on my right hand until I make your foes your footstool."' 2:33-35

At God's right hand, Christ is now reigning as the King over his kingdom. The Holy Spirit had made this promise to him in Psalm 110:1. The promise was made to the Seed, Christ. (Galatians 3:16, 19) He did not receive "the promised Holy Spirit" as in some translations! He was "full of the Holy Spirit" at the beginning of his ministry. (Luke 4:1) Jesus received a throne! The Spirit through the prophet Nathan promised the seed of David, "I will establish the throne of his kingdom." (2 Samuel 7:12-13). In announcing the birth of Jesus to Mary, the angel Gabriel said, "The Lord God shall give to him the throne of his father David." (Luke 1:32). Jesus was raised to sit on David's throne, according to verse 30. At his command, the Holy Spirit's power was poured out upon the apostles, and the people were seeing and hearing miraculous things. The purpose of this power was to establish the kingdom. (Mark 9:1) The Spirit was the means to fulfill the promised kingdom.

"Therefore, let all the house of Israel know assuredly that God has made that same Jesus, whom you have crucified, both Lord and Christ." Now when they heard this, they were pricked in their hearts, and said to Peter and to the rest of the apostles, "Men and brethren, what shall we do?" 2:36-37

Did Peter tell them to call on the name of the Lord or to repeat the Sinner's Prayer? No. He did not.

We should answer this most important question with the same words that were given by the Holy Spirit through Peter. (Acts 2:4)

And Peter said to them, "Repent, and let each of you be baptized in the name of Jesus Christ for the forgiveness of sins; and you shall receive the gift of the Holy Spirit." NASB **2:38**

These believers were instructed to **repent**, which means to change one's way of thinking and purposing. Peter emphasized the importance of baptism by saying, "**and let each of you be baptized** in the name of Jesus Christ **for the forgiveness of sins**." The Greek word translated **baptize** means to immerse. Immersion in water was commanded in Acts 10:47-48 and is described in Acts 8:38-39, where the Ethiopian went down into the water to be immersed, and he came up out of the water.

The baptism is to be **in the name of Jesus Christ.** Those being baptized are to believe in Christ's power, his authority, and all that he is. David Roper says, "They acknowledged their faith in Jesus before they were baptized. The terms 'calls on' in verse 21 and "in the name' in verse 38 weigh heavily on the side of a verbal confession of faith before being baptized." [6] The Greek word translated "in" is not *en* but *epi,* meaning "**upon** the name of Jesus Christ." This is a confession of faith.

The penitent believers were to be baptized **for the remission of sins.** KJV The core meaning of the Greek preposition *eis*, translated "for" in Acts 2:38, is **into**. Baptism is **into** the remission of sins, or "so that sins might be forgiven." [7] The Greek words, *eis aphesin hamartion,* in Acts 2:38 are the same as Jesus' words in Matthew 26:28,

---

[6] David L. Roper, *Truth for Today Commentary, Acts 1-14,* p. 83
[7] Bauer, Arndt, & Gingrich, *A Greek-English Lexicon,* p. 228, sec. 4-f

where he said, "This is My blood of the new covenant, which is shed for many **for the remission of sins**." ^{NKJV} It is in baptism that we come in contact with the blood of Christ that washes away our sins (Rev. 1:7), because we are "baptized into his death." (Rom. 6:3) In baptism we have faith that God is removing our sins. (Col. 2:11-12) If we are to be baptized, as some teach, **because** our sins have already been forgiven, then Jesus shed his blood because our sins were already forgiven. Such teaching denies the atoning sacrifice of Jesus.

"And you shall receive the gift of the Holy Spirit." 2:38

The gift of the Holy Spirit did not come immediately after baptism, but it came when the apostles laid their hands upon baptized believers. (See Lesson 1, pages 3 - 5) The miraculous power of the Holy Spirit was necessary before the writing of the New Testament was completed. The gift of the Holy Spirit enabled new converts to know and teach the gospel and to confirm their message with miracles. (Hebrews 2:3-4) Today, we have the New Testament, which was revealed and confirmed by the gift of the Holy Spirit in the first century. Miraculous gifts are not needed today because "that which is perfect" has come. (1 Cor. 13:8-10). The Greek word *teleion* that is here translated "perfect" means "complete." [8] God's revelation to us has been brought to completion.

For the promise is to you and to your children and to all that are afar off, even as many as the Lord our God shall call." 2:39

We have seen, in Lesson 1, that the promise refers to the one made to Abraham, Isaac, and Jacob, *"And in your seed shall all the nations of the earth be blessed."* The blessing would be not only for the Jews and their children but also for "all that are afar off" – all nations, the Gentiles. And the

---

[8] Wesley J. Perschbacher, *The New Analytical Greek Lexicon*, p. 404

blessing is the forgiveness of sins. (Acts 2:38; Acts 3:25-26; Acts 13:32-28)

And with many other words he did testify and exhort, saying, "Save yourselves from this crooked generation." 2:40

By God's grace we are saved; it is the gift of God. (Eph. 2:8); but God has given conditions for us to receive his gift. We must have faith in Christ, repent of our sins, confess our faith, and be baptized into Christ.

Then they that gladly received his word were baptized; and the same day there were added to them about three thousand souls. 2:41

On Pentecost, three thousand were added to the newly established kingdom of God. In describing "the mysteries of the kingdom," Jesus said, "The seed is the word of God." (Luke 8:10-11) Peter wrote to Christians who were present on Pentecost and said that that they were "born again" of incorruptible seed, "by the word of God which lives and abides forever. And this is the word which by the gospel is preached unto you." (1 Peter 1:23, 25) Jesus taught, "Unless one is born of water and the Spirit, he cannot enter the kingdom of God." NKJV (John 3:5) Before a physical birth, a seed must be received and conceived producing a new life, and a child is born when "the water breaks." In the new birth, the Spirit's word is the seed that must be received and conceived in the mind of a person producing faith and repentance before the new birth is completed when one is baptized in water. Those who were baptized on Pentecost were those that had gladly received the Spirit's word. (Acts 2:41) There must be "the indwelling of the Holy Spirit" before baptism. The Spirit's word produces faith and obedience in us. (Romans 8:5-9; Romans 10:17) Those who have not been baptized have not received the Spirit's word.

And they continued steadfastly in the apostles' doctrine, in fellowship, the breaking of bread, and in prayers. 2:42

The apostles taught them to observe all things that the Lord had commanded. (Matthew 28:20) They shared their new life in Christ. They observed the Lord's Supper. (Matthew 26:26-29 and Luke 22:19-20) They continued in prayers. Roper observes, "When people were baptized, they 'were continually devoting themselves' to worshiping God. Brothers and sisters in Christ worshiped *together*. Nothing is more important." [9]

Fear came upon every soul; and many wonders and signs were done through the apostles. NKJV **2:43**

Everyone was filled with reverence, respect and awe because of the miracles that were done through (Greek, *dia*) the apostles. Through the apostles, believers were able to perform miracles. The apostles laid their hands upon them, and they received miraculous gifts. (Acts 8:14-18; Acts 19:1-6; 1 Corinthians 12:1 – 13:13)

Now all who believed were together, and had all things in common, and sold their possessions and goods, and divided them among all, as anyone had need." NKJV **2:44-45**

They did not sell all their property, because they still had some houses in verse 46. Christians gathered for prayers in the house of Mary the mother of John Mark in Acts 12:12. Sharing their blessings was a demonstration of the fellowship mentioned in verse 42.

And they, continuing daily with one accord in the temple and breaking bread from house to house, did eat their meat with gladness and singleness of heart, praising

---

[9] David L. Roper, *Truth for Today Commentary, Acts 1-14*, p. 95

God and having favor with all the people. And the Lord added to the church daily such as should be saved. 2:46-47

They were meeting daily in the temple for teaching and worship. They were united as they were hearing the "apostles' doctrine."

The "breaking of bread" in verse 42 refers to the Lord's Supper in worship, but in verse 46 it is eating meals together in their houses. The Greek word *trophe* that is translated "meat" in the KJV means "nourishment, food." [10] They enjoyed this time of encouraging each other in the faith as they shared their food.

Souls were being saved every day and added by the Lord to his church/kingdom. The word *ekklesia*, "church," is not in the Greek text, but it is understood. Jesus said to Peter, "I will give to you the keys of the kingdom," immediately after he had said, "I will build my church." (Matthew 16:18, 19) Three thousand souls were added to the church/kingdom on Pentecost when they were saved by accepting of Peter's message and by being baptized. **2:41** Unity in Christ can be enjoyed today if we will preach the same gospel that Peter preached, and if those who receive it are baptized for the remission of sins just like those on Pentecost. The gospel message is not hard to understand, if you sincerely want to know what to do to be saved. The Lord adds all the saved to His church.

---

[10] Wesley J. Perchbacker, *The New Analytical Greek Lexicon*, p. 413

The King's Power to Save
Acts 3:1 – 4:31

Now Peter and John went up together into the temple at the hour of prayer, being the ninth hour. And a certain man lame from his mother's womb was carried, whom they laid daily at the gate of the temple which is called Beautiful, to ask alms of those that entered into the temple; who seeing Peter and John about to go into the temple asked for alms. 3:1-3

The hour of prayer began at our three o'clock in the afternoon; prayers were made while the incense was offered on the golden altar. A man who had never been able to walk in his entire life saw Peter and John and asked for alms.

And Peter fastening his eyes on him with John said, "Look on us." And he gave heed to them expecting to receive something from them. 3:4-5

The crippled man gave them his full attention. Maybe they would give him a generous donation. However, these hopes were soon dashed.

Then Peter said, "Silver and gold I have none; but such as I have, I give you."

What would it be? Just a mite or two? And then to his surprise, Peter said,

"In the name of Jesus Christ of Nazareth rise up and walk." Peter helped him up. **And he took him by the right hand and lifted him up, and immediately his feet and ankle bones received strength. And he leaping up stood, and walked, and entered with them into the temple, walking and leaping, and praising God. 3:6-8**

This man, who had never walked, was instantly and fully healed!

And all the people saw him walking and praising God. And they knew that it was he who sat for alms at the Beautiful Gate of the temple; and they were filled with wonder and amazement at that which had happened to him. And as the lame man who was healed held Peter and John, all the people ran together to them in the porch that is called Solomon's, greatly wondering. 3:9-11

They couldn't believe it. This man who had never walked was now standing with Peter and John in the temple, and everyone wanted to see him. This was an opportunity for Peter to speak about Jesus to a large audience again.

"Men of Israel, why do you marvel at this? Or why look so intently at us, as though by our own power or godliness we had made this man to walk? The God of Abraham, Isaac, and Jacob, the God of our fathers, glorified His Servant Jesus, whom you delivered up and denied in the presence of Pilate, when he was determined to let Him go. But you denied the Holy One and the Just, and asked for a murderer to be granted to you; and killed the Prince of life, whom God has raised from the dead, of which we are witnesses. And His name, through faith in His name, has made this man strong, whom you see and know. Yes, the faith which comes through Him has given him this perfect soundness in the presence of you all." NKJV **3:12-16**

Peter and John did not want any praise or credit for themselves in the healing of the lame man. The God of their fathers had glorified Jesus with this miracle. But the Jews had denied Jesus before Pilate. Peter said that Jesus was God's "Servant" who fulfilled the prophecies in Isaiah 42, 52 and 53. Jesus is "the Holy One," "the Just" and "the Prince of life." They asked for Jesus to be killed instead of a murderer, but God raised Jesus from the dead. Jesus is alive! The apostles were witnesses. They had seen him several times after his resurrection from the dead. Through their faith in the name of Jesus, this well-known lame man was made strong and able to walk.

"And now, brethren, I know that through ignorance you did it, as did your rulers. But those things, which God before had shown by the mouth of all his prophets, that Christ should suffer, he has fulfilled." 3:17

They were expecting a King like David, who would rule over a physical kingdom. They were ignorant of the prophecies predicting that Christ would suffer and die, and then be raised up to bless them with the forgiveness of sins. Premillennialists make the same mistake today, insisting that Christ must have a thousand-year reign upon the earth. His kingdom is a spiritual one. Jesus fulfilled all the prophecies concerning the Christ. (Luke 24:44)

Repent therefore and be converted, that your sins may be blotted out, when times of refreshing shall come from the presence of the Lord. 3:19

These words of Peter parallel his words on Pentecost in Acts 2:38. On both occasions, he called upon his listeners to **repent**. The command to **be converted** describes what takes place when one obeys the command to "**be baptized** in the name of Jesus Christ." Conversion takes place when we are baptized into Christ's death" (Romans 6:3) and are raised "through faith in the operation of God" to remove our sins (Colossians 2:11-12). God raises us up from the waters of baptism to walk in newness of life." (Romans 6:4) The promise that your **sins may be blotted out** is "**the remission** of sins." The **times of refreshing** refer to "**the gift of the Holy Spirit**." Jesus had said, "If any man is thirsty, let him come to Me and drink. He who believes in me, as the Scripture said, 'From his innermost being will flow rivers of living water.'" John by inspiration of the Holy Spirit says, "But this He spoke of the Spirit, whom those who believed in Him were to receive, for the Spirit was not yet given, because Jesus was not yet glorified." ᴺᴬˢᴮ (John 7:37-39) The gift of the Holy Spirit was not given until the day of Pentecost; but before then, the Spirit was working in his divine providence and in his answering prayers. Thus, the gift of the Holy Spirit cannot be answered prayers and the Spirit's providential working in our lives. The gift is the revelation of Christ's gospel. The inspired words of the New Testament are like refreshing rivers of water; they **renew** us. Christians are **not** transformed by a personal indwelling of the Holy Spirit keeping them from sinning. We are not the incarnation of God the Spirit! The apostle Paul admonishes, "And be not conformed to this world, but be ye transformed by the **renewing of your mind**, that you may prove what is that good, and acceptable and perfect will of God." (Rom. 12:2) We do this by reading the New Testament and applying its teachings to our lives. "The truth is in Jesus: that you put off, concerning the old man which grows corrupt according to deceitful lust, and **be renewed in the spirit of your mind,** and that you put on the new man which was created according to God, in true righteousness and holiness." ᴺᴷᴶⱽ (Ephesians 4:21-24) Just as the heavenly Father and Christ dwell in us figuratively, so the Spirit also dwells in us figuratively through his word, the Bible. We are not God incarnated.

"And he shall send Jesus Christ, who before was preached to you, whom the heaven must receive until the times of restitution of all things, which God has spoken by the mouth of all his holy prophets since the world began." 3:20-21

When Jesus Christ returns, all predictions of God's prophets will be completely realized. The "restoration of all things" is limited to the things God has spoken by the mouth of his holy prophets.

"For Moses truly said to the fathers, 'The LORD your God will raise up for you a Prophet like me from your brethren. Him you shall hear in all things, whatever he says to you. And it shall be that every soul who will not hear that Prophet shall be utterly destroyed from among the people.' Yes, and all the prophets, from Samuel and those who follow, as many as have spoken, have also foretold these days." NKJV **3:22-24**

Peter quoted Deuteronomy 18:15-19. In addition to being a prophet, Moses also was a deliverer and a lawgiver. Jesus said, "Had you believed Moses, you would believe me, for he wrote of me." (John 5:46) All the prophets predicted the days of Christ and his kingdom.

"Ye are the children of the prophets and of the covenant which God made with our fathers, saying to Abraham, 'And in your seed all the families of the earth shall be blessed.' ... God, having raised up his Son Jesus, sent him to bless you in turning away every one of you from your iniquities." 3:25

This is "the promise made to the fathers" that is mentioned often in the book of Acts. (See Lesson 1, pages 6-7.) The blessing is the forgiveness of sins. Christ the King has the power to blot out and erase our sins.

And as they spoke to the people, the priests, and the captain of the temple, and the Sadducees came upon them, being grieved that they taught the people, and preached through Jesus the resurrection of the dead. And they laid hands on them and put them in hold to the next day, for it was now eventide. 4:1-3

The persecution against the church by the Jewish leaders had begun. The priests were in charge of teaching in the temple, and they felt that the apostles had no right to be preaching in the temple. (Luke 20:1-2) Sadducees were offended by Peter's preaching, because they denied the resurrection of the dead. (Luke 20:29) Jesus had warned his disciples, "They will lay their hands on you and persecute you, delivering you up to the synagogues and prisons. You will be brought before kings and rulers for My name's sake. But it will turn out for you as an occasion for testimony." NKJV (Luke 21:12-13)

Many of them which heard the word believed; and the number of men was about five thousand. 4:4

The church/kingdom was growing rapidly. The healing of the crippled beggar had caused many to believe and obey the gospel of Christ.

The next day the rulers, elders and teachers of the law met in Jerusalem. Annas the high priest was there, and so were Caiaphas, John Alexander and other members of the high priest's family. They had Peter and John brought before them and began to question them: "By what power or what name did you do this?" NIV 4:5-6

This was the same Sanhedrin (Council) that had condemned Jesus to death. These Jewish rulers wanted to know by what power Peter and John had performed this great miracle. Name is used for power.

Then Peter, filled with the Holy Spirit, said to them, "You rulers of the people and elders of Israel: If we this day be examined of the good deed done to the impotent man, by what manner he is made whole; be it known to you all, and to all the people of Israel, that by the name of Jesus Christ of Nazareth, whom you crucified, whom God raised from the dead, even by him does this man stand here before you whole. This is the 'stone which was rejected by you builders, which is become the head of the corner.' Neither is there salvation in any other, for there is none other name under heaven given among men by which we must be saved." 4:8-12

The Holy Spirit was speaking through Peter, and he boldly proclaimed that Jesus of Nazareth is the Christ, the Anointed King. All the people should know that Jesus Christ is the power that made the lame man walk; and only in His name is salvation. The Anointed King has power to save men's souls from eternal damnation and give to them eternal life.

Now when they saw the boldness of Peter and John, and perceived that they were unlearned and ignorant men, they marveled; and they took knowledge of them that they had been with Jesus. And beholding the man which was healed standing with them, they could say nothing against it. But when they had commanded them to go aside out of the council, they conferred among themselves, saying, "What shall we do to these men? For that indeed a notable miracle is manifest to all that dwell in Jerusalem; and we cannot deny it. 4:13-16

The Jews could not deny this great miracle, nor could they deny the boldness and power being demonstrated in these uneducated apostles of Jesus. **4:15-16**

Then they called them in again and commanded them not to speak or teach at all in the name of Jesus. But Peter and John replied, "Judge for yourselves whether it is right in God's sight to obey you rather than God. For we cannot help speaking about what we have seen and heard." NIV **4:18-20**

Peter and John gave us a good example to follow. We must listen to God. The word of God is our absolute authority. Christ is on the throne!

After further threats they let them go. They could not decide how to punish them, because all the people were praising God for what had happened. For the man who was miraculously healed was over forty years old. On their release, Peter and John went back to their own people and reported all that the chief priests and elders had said to them. NIV **4:21-23**

The court released the apostles without punishment, because the people were praising God for the great miracle of giving the power to walk to a man who had never been able to walk in his entire life of forty years! Peter and John reported to the other apostles and brethren of the threats being made against them by the Sanhedrin.

When they heard this, they raised their voices together in prayer to God. "Sovereign Lord," they said, "you made the heaven and the earth and the sea, and everything in them. You spoke through the mouth of your servant David:

'Why did the nations rage,
    and the people plot in vain?
The kings of the earth take their stand
    and the rulers gather together against the Lord
    and against his Anointed One.'

In deed Herod and Pontius Pilate met together with the Gentiles and the people of Israel in this city to conspire against your holy servant Jesus, whom you anointed. They did what your power and will had decided beforehand should happen. Now, Lord, consider their threats and enable your servants to speak your word with great boldness. Stretch out your hand to heal and perform miraculous signs and wonders through the name of our holy servant Jesus."

After they prayed, the place where they were meeting was shaken. And they were all filled with the Holy Spirit and spoke the word of God boldly. ^{NIV} 4:23-31

United in prayer, the brethren applied Psalm Two to Jesus. Then they prayed for boldness to speak God's word and for miracles to show Christ's power. And the place where they were assembled was shaken. God was answering their prayer. Being filled with the Holy Spirit they were empowered to boldly proclaim God's word.

NOTES

The Apostles Are Witnesses
Acts 4:32 – 5:42

And with great power the apostles gave witness of the resurrection of the Lord Jesus, and great grace was upon them all. 4:33

Jesus had said to his apostles just before his ascension into heaven. "You shall be witnesses unto me both in Jerusalem and in all Judea, and in Samaria, and unto the uttermost part of the earth." (1:8) We now see the apostles bearing witness to Jesus and his resurrection in Jerusalem.

And the multitude of them that believed were of one heart and of one soul: neither said any of them that any of the things which he possessed was his own; but they had all things in common. 4:32 Neither was there any among them that lacked. For as many as were possessors of land or houses sold them and brought the prices of the things sold and laid them down at the apostles' feet, and distribution was made to every man according as he had need. 4:34-35

The believers were united in one heart. They looked at their possessions as belonging to God. Their generosity is explained by J. W. McGarvey: "This was not the result of socialistic theorizing or of rules laid down to govern all, but it was the spontaneous expression of the love of God and man which had taken possession of every heart." [11] The prayer of Jesus "that they all may be one" was being answered. (John 17:21) Jesus had said, "By this all men shall know that you are my disciples, if you have love one to another." (John 13:35)

---

[11] J. W. McGarvey, *New Commentary on Acts of Apostles*, p. 79

Thus Joseph, who was also called by the apostles Barnabas (which means Son of Encouragement), a Levite, a native of Cyprus, sold a field that belonged to him and brought the money and laid it at the apostles' feet. ESV **4:36-37**

Barnabas would be Paul's traveling companion on his first missionary journey. The apostles gave him the name Barnabas, because he was known for his encouraging and comforting others. He brought the money from the sale of his field and gave it to the apostles for distribution among the needy.

But a certain man named Ananias, with Sapphira, his wife, sold a possession. And he kept back part of the proceeds, his wife also being aware of it, and brought a certain part and laid it at the apostles' feet. But Peter said, "Ananias, why has Satan filled your heart to lie to the Holy Spirit and keep back part of the price of the land for yourself? While it remained, was it not your own? And after it was sold, was it not in your control? Why have you conceived this thing in your heart? You have not lied to men but to God." NKJV **5:1-4**

Ananias and his wife wanted others to think they were giving all of the proceeds from the sale of their land to the apostles. But the Holy Spirit revealed their deception to Peter. The Spirit was the power and authority behind Peter's words and actions. Lying to Peter was lying to the Holy Spirit. Peter clearly states that the selling of lands and houses by the brethren was completely voluntary. The right of ownership of private property was not being questioned. He said that the land and the money belonged to them to do with as they wished. But Jesus had warned his disciples of the danger of doing charitable deeds to be seen of men (Matthew 6:1) Their sin was lying to God.

> Then Ananias, hearing these words, fell down and breathed his last. So great fear came upon all those who heard these things. And young men arose and wrapped him up, carried him out, and buried him. Now it was about three hours later when his wife came in, not knowing what had happened. And Peter answered her, "Tell me whether you sold the land for so much?" She said, "Yes, for so much." Then Peter said to her, "How is it that you have agreed to test the Spirit of the Lord? Look, the feet of those who have buried your husband are at the door, and they will carry you out." Then immediately she fell down at his feet and breathed her last. And the young men came in and found her dead, and carrying her out, buried her by her husband. ^{NKJV} **5:5-11**

God knows if we are being truthful. The Holy Spirit was giving revelation and power to the apostles. He was guiding them "into all truth" just as Jesus had promised. (John 16:13) Ananias and his wife could not hide their sin from the apostles, because God was inspiring them with the truth. They were lying to God.

> **And through the hands of the apostles many signs and wonders were done among the people. And they were all with one accord in Solomon's porch. Yet none of the rest dared join them, but the people esteemed them highly.** ^{NKJV} **5:12-13**

The Greek preposition *dia* means "through" and expresses "the intermediate agent through whom the original agent acts." [12] The hands of the apostles were the intermediate agent through which the Holy Spirit gave miraculous gifts to believers. (8:14-18)

---

[12] David Alan Black, *Learn to Read New Testament Greek*, p. 81

The church was meeting at the temple. Roper explains **5:13**, "These who might have 'joined the church' merely for what they could get out of it did not dare to associate with them." [13] God's punishment for the sin of lying purified the church.

And believers were increasingly added to the Lord, multitudes of both men and women. 5:14 Also a multitude gathered from surrounding cities to Jerusalem, bringing sick folks, and those that were tormented by unclean spirits, and they were all healed. NKJV **5:16**

The church was growing and having favor with the people even from beyond Jerusalem. Christ's power was being demonstrated by the Holy Spirit through the apostles.

Then the high priest rose up, and all those who were with him (which is the sect of the Sadducees), and they were filled with indignation, and laid their hands on the apostles and put them in the common prison. But at night an angel of the Lord opened the prison doors and brought them out, and said, "Go, stand in the temple and speak to the people all the words of this life." NKJV **5:17-20**

The apostles were not released from prison for their safety but in order to teach in the name of Jesus. With faith and courage, the apostles **entered into the temple early in the morning and taught. 5:21** While they were teaching, the high priest called the Sanhedrin together for their trial. But when the officers went to the prison to bring the apostles to the council, they found the prison was secure and the guards were standing before the doors. But the apostles were gone. When the Jewish leaders heard these things, **they wondered what the outcome would be.** NKJV **5:21-24** They had no power over the apostles. Large crowds were gathering to hear the apostles teach about Jesus. Instead of acknowledging that

---

[13] David L. Roper, *Truth for Today Commentary, Acts 1-14*, p. 193

God's power was with the apostles, the priests were afraid of losing their place as teachers in the temple.

Then one came and told them, saying, "Behold, the men whom you put in prison are standing in the temple and teaching the people." Then the captain went with the officers and brought them without violence, for they feared the people lest they should have been stoned. 5:25-26

The arresting officers were afraid for their own safety, because the apostles were in favor with the people. The apostles went to their trial before the Sanhedrin, and they had another opportunity to be witnesses for Jesus.

And the high priest asked them, saying, "Did not we straitly command you that ye should not to teach in this name? And, behold, ye have filled Jerusalem with your doctrine, and intend to bring this man's blood upon us!" 5:27-28

Caiaphas was the high priest who was speaking, and he was the high priest who had called for the death of Jesus. (John 11:49-50; John 18:13-14; Matthew 26:62-66) He was guilty of the blood of Jesus! When they wanted Jesus crucified. they had cried out, "His blood be on us." Jesus proved his innocence by his resurrection and by the power of the Holy Spirit that was being demonstrated through his apostles. (Romans 1:1-4, 11)

Then Peter and the other apostles answered and said, "We ought to obey God rather than men." 5:29

God had miraculously delivered the apostles from prison with the command to speak in the temple all the words of life. (5:19-20) We are to obey the governing authorities. (Romans 13:1-7) However, God's power and authority is greater. Anytime man's laws and regulations differ from God's teachings, we are to obey God.

Peter testified, **"The God of our fathers raised up Jesus, whom ye slew and hanged on a tree. God has exalted Him with his own right hand to be a Prince and a Savior, for to give repentance to Israel and forgiveness of sins. We are his witnesses of these things, and so is the Holy Spirit, whom God has given to them that obey him. 5:30-32**

These rulers of the Jews were guilty of crucifying Jesus, but his resurrection from the dead was God's way to lead them to repentance and the forgiveness of their sins. Peter testified that he and the other apostles had seen Jesus after his resurrection. When Jesus was arrested, these were the same men who fled and forsook him. Peter had even denied knowing Jesus. What had transformed them from cowards, hiding in locked rooms, to fearless men who were boldly proclaiming their faith in Jesus before the same council that had condemned Jesus to death? The answer is evident. They had seen Jesus, who was alive from the dead. God has exalted him to his own right hand as the Christ. He has power and authority over the Sanhedrin. He is our King and Savior.

Peter said that the Holy Spirit was also a witness to the resurrection of Jesus? (5:32) Jesus had said, "The Spirit of truth, who proceeds from the Father, he shall testify of me." (John 15:26) How did the Holy Spirit testify of Jesus and serve as a witness to His resurrection? It was not, as some teach, by a non-miraculous personal indwelling of the Holy Spirit that is given to all obedient believers. What kind of proof of the resurrection would that have been before the Sanhedrin? The witness of the Holy Spirit was the undeniable miraculous power that could be seen in church during the first century. The apostles had the Holy Spirit's power, and also obedient believers received the Spirit's power when an apostle laid his hands upon them. (Acts 8:5-17; Acts 19:1-6)

Let's not replace God's miraculous proof with human feelings!

When they heard that, they were cut to the heart, and took counsel to slay them. 5:33

The word of God is described as a "two-edged sword" that "is a discerner of the thoughts and intents of the heart." (Hebrews 4:12) The word of God cut the hearts of the three thousand on the day of Pentecost, and they believed and obeyed the gospel. The same word cut the hearts of these Jewish rulers, and they wanted to kill the apostles.

But a Pharisee in the council named Gamaliel, a teacher of the law held in honor by all the people, stood up and gave orders to put the men outside for a little while. And he said to them, "Men of Israel, take care what you are about to do with these men. For before these days Theudas rose up, claiming to be somebody, and a number of men, about four hundred, joined him. He was killed, and all who followed him were dispersed and came to nothing. After him Judas the Galilean rose up in the days of the census and drew away some of the people after him. He too perished, and all who followed him scattered. So in this present case I tell you, keep away from these men and let them alone, for if this plan or this undertaking is of man, it will fail; but if it is of God, you will not be able to overthrow them. You might even be found opposing God!" ESV 5:34-39

The apostle Paul was a student of this famous teacher. (Acts 22:3) Gamaliel reminded the council of Theudas and Judas of Galilee, who for a time had many followers, but their causes came to nothing. He advised the council to leave the apostles alone. David Lipscomb wrote, "These men (the apostles) had shown divine power. So while Gamaliel was not a believer, he was so impressed with the possibility that they might be sent by God that he was unwilling for the Sanhedrin to try to destroy them." [14]   Roper advises us, "When someone teaches error, God does not want us to use *violence* to suppress that error; rather, God would have us oppose error with *truth*." [15]

And to him they agreed; and when they had called the apostles and beaten them, they commanded that they should not speak in the name of Jesus and let them go. And they departed from the presence of the council, rejoicing that they were counted worthy to suffer shame for his name. And daily in the temple and in every house, they ceased not to teach and preach Jesus Christ. 5:40-42

Persecution could not stop the preaching of the gospel of Christ. Jesus had said to his disciples, "Blessed are they who are persecuted for righteousness' sake, for theirs is the kingdom of heaven. Blessed are ye, when men shall revile you and persecute you and shall say all manner of evil against you falsely, for my sake. Rejoice, and be exceedingly glad, for great is your reward in heaven." (Matthew 5:10-12)

---

[14] David Lipscomb, *A Commentary on the Acts of the Apostles,* p. 71
[15] David L. Roper, *Truth for Today Commentary, Acts 1-14,* p. 207

The First Christian Martyr
Acts 6:1 – 8:3

And in those days, when the number of the disciples was multiplied, there arose a murmuring of the Grecians against the Hebrews, because their widows were neglected in the daily ministration. 6:1

The "Grecians" were Jews from countries outside of Palestine, whose first language was Greek, the universal language. Some of them may have stayed after Pentecost to hear more of the apostles' teachings. Also, Jews from other nations had come to Jerusalem to live, and they had their own Jewish synagogue. (6:9) The "Hebrews" were Palestinian Jews, whose daily language was a version of Hebrew, called Aramaic. The Greek-speaking Christians were saying that their widows were being neglected in the daily serving of food. This problem was threatening the unity of the church. (Acts 4:32)

Then the twelve called the multitude of the disciples, and said, "It is not reasonable that we should leave the word of God and serve tables. Therefore, brethren, you look out among you seven men of honest report, full of the Holy Spirit and wisdom, whom we may appoint over this business. But we will give ourselves to the ministry of the word." And the saying pleased the whole multitude; and they chose Stephen, a man full of faith and of the Holy Spirit, and Philip and Prochorus and Nicanor and Timon and Parmenas and Nicolas, a proselyte of Antioch, whom they set before the apostles. And when they had prayed, they laid their hands on them. 6:2-6

The disciples in Jerusalem may have grown to over twenty thousand members by this time. Each part of the body of Christ has a special work to do. (Romans 12:4-8) The work of the apostles was teaching and preaching and prayer. The apostles gave the qualifications for seven men to serve tables, and they let the church make the selection. The seven men to serve tables had to be of **honest report, full of the Holy Spirit and wisdom.**

What does it mean to be full of the Holy Spirit? When Jesus was "full of the Holy Spirit" he had miraculous power; the devil was able to tempt Jesus because he had the power to turn stones into bread. (Luke 4:1-4) Stephen and Philip were among the seven chosen to serve tables, because they both were full of the Holy Spirit and could work miracles. (Acts 6:8; Acts 8:5-7) The gift of the Holy Spirit was received by baptized believers (Acts 2:38), but they did not receive the gift until apostles laid their hands on them (Acts 8:12, 14-18). The gift of the Holy Spirit involved various gifts. There were "diversities of gifts, but the same Spirit," according to 1 Corinthians 12:4. And the first one mentioned in 1 Corinthians 12:8 was the gift of "wisdom." One needed to be full of the Holy Spirit and wisdom in order to serve tables.

Another purpose of the laying on of hands was to appoint men to a work. When Paul and Barnabas were appointed to their mission work, the church in Antioch of Syria "fasted and prayed, and laid their hands on them." (Acts 13:2-3) Timothy was appointed to preach with the laying on of the hands of the elders (1 Timothy 4:14), but he received the gift of prophecy through (Gk., *dia*) the laying on of the apostle Paul's hands. (2 Timothy 1:6)

The church was to select "seven men of honest report, full of the Holy Spirit and wisdom," whom the apostles could **appoint over this business.** It is inferred that the seven men had received the gift of the Holy Spirit before the apostles appointed them to this work. They were already "full of the

Holy Spirit and wisdom." The apostles appointed them to serve tables by praying and laying their hands on them. **6:6** Let the Bible speak.

All seven men appointed to serve tables had Greek names, indicating they spoke Greek, which also would help them in their work.

The word of God increased; and the number of disciples multiplied in Jerusalem greatly; and a great company of the priests were obedient to the faith. 6:7

The spiritual body of Christ was growing because they were speaking the truth in love and working together with each member doing his share. (Ephesians 4:15-16) Even a great number of the priests obeyed the gospel by repenting and being baptized for the remission of sins. (Acts 2:38, 41) Roper states, "These **priests** probably would not have been the 'chief priests' who were persecuting the apostles (4:23; 5:24), but rather the 'ordinary priests' who served in the temple two weeks out of the year." [16] Like Zacharias, the father of John the Baptist, they had honest hearts that feared God. Their conversions testified to the power of the gospel of Christ.

And Stephen, full of grace and power, was doing great wonders and signs among the people. Then some of those who belonged to the synagogue of the Freedmen, (as it was called), and of the Cyrenians, and of the Alexandrians, and of those from Cilicia and Asia, rose up and disputed with Stephen. But they could not withstand the wisdom and the Spirit with which he was speaking. ᴱˢⱽ **6:8-10**

Saul of Tarsus, Cilicia, probably was among those disputing with Stephen. (Acts 22:3) Stephen may have been a member of this synagogue before his conversion. Stephen

---

[16] David L. Roper, *Truth for Today Commentary, Acts 1-14*, p. 235

demonstrated the wisdom given him by the Spirit and had qualified him to serve tables. The word *Spirit* is capitalized in most translations, meaning the Holy Spirit. Stephen had the gift of prophecy inspiring him to speak. The Holy Spirit's power could be seen in him.

Then they secretly induced men who said, "We have heard him speak blasphemous words against Moses and against God." 6:11

The Freemen were Pharisees, and they no doubt were concerned because the church was having favor with many who were Pharisees. They accused Stephen of speaking slanderous words against Moses and God.

And they stirred up the people and the elders and the scribes. And they came upon him and caught him and brought him to the council. And they set up false witnesses, who said, "This man ceases not to speak blasphemous words against this holy place and the law. For we have heard him say that this Jesus of Nazareth shall destroy this place and shall change the customs which Moses delivered us." And all that sat in the council, looking steadfastly on him, saw his face as it had been the face of an angel. 6:12-15

Jesus had predicted the destruction of the temple and Jerusalem (Matthew 24:1-2); and he had fulfilled the Law with his perfect sacrifice and new covenant. Stephen looked calm and confident, as an angel of God.

Stephen's Sermon to the Sanhedrin

Then the high priest said, "Are these things so?" And he said, "The God of glory appeared to our father Abraham, when he was in Mesopotamia, before he dwelt in Haran, and said to him, 'Get out of your country and

from your kindred, and come into the land which I will show you.'" 7:1-3

The witnesses had accused Stephen of slandering God, but he begins his message by speaking of "The God of glory," and his last words describe the glory of God. (7:56) He reviews their history, beginning with Abraham.

Abraham left his kindred in the land of the Chaldeans and came to Haran, where his father died. God's first call to Abraham was in Ur of the Chaldeans. (Genesis 15:7) The second call was in Haran, and Abraham went to the land of Canaan. (Genesis 11:31 – 12:5) Abraham was not given the land at that time, but God promised it to him and to his descendants for a possession. But at that time, Abraham had no child. **7:4-5**

God told Abraham that his descendants would be in a foreign land (Egypt) and be in bondage for four hundred years. God said he would judge that nation and deliver Abraham's people. They would then serve God in the land he had promised them. **7:6-7**

God gave Abraham the covenant of circumcision. When Abraham begot Isaac, he circumcised him on the eighth day. Isaac begot Jacob, and Jacob begot the twelve patriarchs.

"And the patriarchs, moved with envy, sold Joseph into Egypt; but God was with him, and delivered him out of all his afflictions, and gave him favor and wisdom in the sight of Pharaoh king of Egypt, and he made him governor over Egypt." 7:9-10

Roper notes, "As Stephen spoke of the patriarchs, he introduced a new theme. Throughout the Jew's history, they had *rejected* God's appointed deliverers. The first God-appointed deliverer rejected by their fathers was Joseph." [17]

---

[17] David L. Roper, *Truth for Today Commentary, Acts 1-14*, p. 255

But God was with Joseph, who became a ruler and was able to save his people during a great famine.

During a famine, Jacob heard that there was grain in Egypt, and he sent his sons there to buy grain. The second time they came to Egypt, Joseph made himself known to his brothers, and they were made known to Pharaoh. Joseph's family of seventy-five persons came to live with him in Egypt. Jacob and his sons died in Egypt, but their bodies were carried back to Canaan for burial. **7:11-16**

"But when the time of the promise drew near which God had sworn to Abraham, the people grew and multiplied in Egypt till another king arose who did not know Joseph. This man dealt treacherously with our people ... making them expose their babies, so that they might not live.

"At this time Moses was born, and was well pleasing to God; and he was brought up in his father's house for three months. But when he was set out, Pharaoh's daughter took him and brought him up as her own son. And Moses was learned in all the wisdom of the Egyptians, and was mighty in words and deeds." NKJV **7:17-22**

Although Moses was the adopted son of Pharaoh's daughter, his own mother was his nurse and teacher during his early formative years. (Exodus 2:7-10) And being educated by the Egyptians, Moses became known for his eloquent speech and his achievements.

"Now when he was forty years old, it came into his heart to visit his brethren, the children of Israel. And seeing one of them suffer wrong, he defended and avenged him who was oppressed, and struck down the Egyptian. For he supposed his brethren would have understood that

God would deliver them by his hand, but they did not understand. And the next day he appeared to two of them as they were fighting, and tried to reconcile them, saying, 'Men, you are brethren; why do you wrong one another?' But he that did his neighbor wrong pushed him away, saying, 'Who made you a ruler and a judge over us? Do you want to kill me as you did the Egyptian yesterday?' Then, at this saying, Moses fled and became a dweller in the land of Midian, where he had two sons." NKJV 7:23-29

When Moses was forty years old, he thought God would use him to deliver his people from their slavery in Egypt. But he was rejected by the people of Israel. Moses fled to the land of Midian, where he married Zipporah and had children. (Exodus 2:14-22) For the next forty years, Moses would be a shepherd in a foreign land.

"*And when forty years had passed, an Angel of the Lord appeared to him in a flame of fire in a bush in the wilderness of Mount Sinai. When Moses saw it, he marveled at the sight; and as he drew near to observe, the voice of the Lord came to him, saying, 'I am the God of your fathers—the God of Abraham, and the God of Isaac, and the God of Jacob.' And Moses trembled and dared not look. Then the* L<small>ORD</small> *said to him, 'Take your sandals off your feet, for the place where you stand is holy ground. I have surely seen the oppression of My people who are in Egypt; I have heard their groanings and have come down to deliver them. And now come, I will send you to Egypt.'*" NKJV 7:30-34

The word Angel is capitalized because he said, "I am the **God of your fathers.**" *Angel* **means "messenger."** Before he was made flesh, Jesus existed in eternity as the Word. (John 1:1-14) He is the member of the divine Trinity who speaks to man. Stephen is emphasizing their fathers' rejection of Moses, whom God had sent to be their deliverer and lawgiver.

"This Moses whom they rejected, saying, 'Who made you a ruler and a judge?' is the one God sent to be a ruler and deliverer by the hand of the Angel who appeared to him in the bush. He brought them out, after he had shown wonders and signs in the land of Egypt, and in the Red Sea, and in the wilderness forty years. This is that Moses, who said to the children of Israel, 'The LORD your God will raise up for you a Prophet like me from your brethren. Him you shall hear.'" NKJV **7:35-37**

Jesus is the Prophet like Moses. God sent him to be our deliverer and ruler. His miraculous signs were even greater than Moses. Their fathers refused Moses, and the Jews had rejected Jesus.

"This is he who was in the congregation in the wilderness with the Angel who spoke to him on Mount Sinai, and with our fathers, the one who received the living oracles to give to us, whom our fathers would not obey, but rejected. And in their hearts turned back to Egypt, saying to Aaron, 'Make us gods to go before us; as for this Moses who brought us out of the land of Egypt, we do not know what has become of him.' And they made a calf in those days, and offered sacrifice to the idol, and rejoiced in the works of their own hands." NKJV **7:38-41**

Moses was with the congregation of Israel in the wilderness. The Angel of God's Presence was guiding and protecting them on their journey. (Ex. 14:19; 33:19) Stephen said "the Angel" spoke to Moses on Mount Sinai and with our fathers. Moses received "the living oracles," the Ten Commandments, for them to obey. Their fathers not only rejected Moses, but also the LORD God and his living word for a lifeless golden calf, an idol—the works of their own hands. They immediately disobeyed the first two Commandments: *"Thou shalt have no other gods before me. Thou shalt not make unto thee any graven image ... Thou shalt not bow down thyself to them or serve them."* (Ex. 20:3-4)

Stephen is pointing out that the nation of Israel had rejected God, Moses and the Law from its time in the wilderness.

"Then God turned and gave them up to worship the host of heaven, as it is written in the Prophets:

> *'Did you offer Me slaughtered animals and*
> *sacrifices during forty years in the wilderness,*
> *O house of Israel?*
> *You also took up the tabernacle of Moloch,*
> *And the star of Remphan* (Saturn)*,*
> *Images which you made to worship;*
> *And I will carry you away beyond Babylon.'"*
> _{NKJV} **7:42-43**

Stephen refers to Amos 5:25-27 to show how God, in the past, had rejected Israel for rejecting Him. The Assyrians scattered the northern tribes beyond Damascus, and the Chaldeans carried away the southern tribes beyond Babylon. The prophets had predicted their punishment for their idolatry.

"Our fathers had the tabernacle of witness in the wilderness, as He appointed, instructing Moses to make it according to the pattern he had seen, which our fathers ... brought with Joshua into the land possessed by the Gentiles." _{NKJV} **7:44-45**

Stephen is now answering the charge that he had spoken against the temple. God had instructed Moses how to make the tabernacle. God's presence was represented by the Most Holy Place with the Ark of the Covenant.

"But Solomon built him a house. However, the Most High dwells not in temples made with hands, as the prophet says, 'Heaven is my throne, and earth is my footstool. What house will you build me?' says the Lord, 'or what is the place of my rest? Has not my hand made all these things?'" 7:46-50

This quotation is from Isaiah 66:1-2. God rules from his throne in heaven. The Creator of all things does not need men to build his temple. The church is God's spiritual temple today. (1 Cor. 3:16; Ephesians 2:19-22) Stephen concluded with these words of condemnation.

"You stiff-necked and uncircumcised in hearts and ears, you do resist the Holy Spirit; as your fathers did, so do you." 7:51

They were prejudiced and stubborn. Their hearts and ears were like uncircumcised Gentiles. They were defiled and hardened with the desires of the flesh. Roper states, "They had accused Stephen of not respecting God, but they themselves were resisting **the Holy Spirit** (see Isaiah 63:10) by not listening to those who spoke by the power of the Spirit (2 Peter 1:21). When men today reject the gospel, they also are resisting the Holy Spirit." [18]

"Which of the prophets have not your fathers persecuted? And they killed them who showed before the coming of the Just One, of whom you have been now the betrayers and murderers, who have received the law by the direction of angels, and have not kept it." 7:52-53

They accused Stephen of speaking against the law (6:13), but they had not kept it. His words cut like a sword. But instead of repenting of their sins, they wanted to kill him.

---

[18] David L. Roper, *Truth for Today Commentary, Acts 1-14*, p. 266

When they heard these things, they were cut to the heart, and they gnashed on him with their teeth. But he, being full of the Holy Spirit, looked up steadfastly into heaven and saw the glory of God, and Jesus standing on the right hand of God, and said, "Behold! I see the heavens opened, and the Son of man standing on the right hand of God." 7:54-56

What a witness! Instead of fear and dread on his face, there was joy and excitement of seeing Jesus! If we also are faithful, we can have that same joy and expectation of seeing Jesus.

Then they cried out with a loud voice, and stopped their ears, and ran upon him with one accord, and cast him out of the city, and stoned him. And the witnesses laid down their clothes at a young man's feet, whose name was Saul. 7:57-58

Saul was consenting to the death of Stephen. (8:1) Luke is reporting the testimony of an eye-witness, Saul of Tarsus. Luke was a close friend and traveling companion of Saul, who became the apostle Paul.[19] The words of Stephen and his calm, forgiving manner as he faced death must have been hard for Saul to forget. They may have been among the goads that were pricking him as he persecuted the church. (26:14)

And they stoned Stephen, calling upon God, and saying, "Lord Jesus, receive my spirit." And he knelt down and cried with a loud voice, "Lord, lay not this sin to their charge." And when he had said this, he fell asleep. And Saul was consenting to his death. And at that time there was a great persecution against the church which was at Jerusalem; and they were all scattered abroad throughout the regions of Judea and Samaria, except the

---

[19] John W. Wade, *Acts*, p. 68

apostles. And devout men carried Stephen to his burial and made great lamentation over him. 7:59 – 8:2

Stephen died as the first martyr for Christ. The word *martyr* literally means "witness." He died as a witness to his faith in Jesus.

But Saul was ravaging the church, and entering house after house, he dragged off men and women and committed them to prison. ᴱˢⱽ **8:3**

Many more Christians would suffer and die for their faith in Jesus Christ.

Philip the Evangelist
Acts 8:4-40

Therefore, they that were scattered abroad went everywhere preaching the word. 8:4

Saul's efforts to silence the church in Jerusalem caused the gospel to spread throughout Judea and Samaria. God uses persecutions against his people as opportunities for them to proclaim their faith in him. (Luke 21:12-13; Acts 5:27-32; Daniel 3:13-28)

Then Philip went down to the city of Samaria and preached Christ to them. And the people with one accord gave heed to those things which Philip spoke, hearing and seeing the miracles which he did. For unclean spirits, crying with loud voices, came out of many that were possessed with them; and many taken with palsies and that were lame were healed. And there was great joy in the city. 8:5-8

Philip was one of the seven appointed to serve tables in Jerusalem. (Acts 6:2-5) When the persecution came, he became an evangelist, proclaiming Christ as the King. His divinely inspired message was confirmed by various miracles.

But there was a certain man called Simon, who previously practiced sorcery in the city and astonished the people of Samaria, claiming that he was someone great, to whom they all gave heed, from the least to the greatest, saying, "This man is the great power of God." And they heeded him because he had astonished them with his sorceries for a long time. But when they believed Philip as he preached the things concerning the kingdom of God and the name of Jesus Christ, they were baptized, both men and women. NKJV **8:9-12**

Philip declared the authority of Jesus Christ as King over his kingdom. His miracles testified to the power of Christ. The Samaritans entered the kingdom of God when they believed and were baptized. (John 3:5) Philip was reaping a harvest of souls. Jesus had sown the seeds of the kingdom in Samaria earlier when he visited with the woman at Jacob's well. (John 4:4-42) The Samaritans were a mixed people, part Israelites and part Gentiles. They believed in the true God of Israel, but they did not worship in Jerusalem but on Mt. Gerizim. (John 4:20)

Then Simon himself believed also; and when he was baptized, he continued with Philip and wondered, beholding the miracles and signs which were done. 8:13

Philip's true miracles of God tested the magic of Simon. Even Simon was convinced when he saw the great power of the Holy Spirit. Some people question Simon's conversion, but Luke was being guided by the Holy Spirit when he wrote about Simon. Jesus had said, "He that believes and is baptized shall be saved." (Mark 16:16)

Now when the apostles who were at Jerusalem heard that Samaria had received the word of God, they sent to them Peter and John, who when they were come down, prayed for them that they might receive the Holy Spirit. (For as yet he was fallen upon none of them; only they were baptized in the name of the Lord Jesus.) 8:14-16

On the day of Pentecost, Peter promised "and you shall receive the gift of the Holy Spirit." (Acts 2:38) However, Peter did not tell them **when** or **how** they would receive the gift. The Samaritans did not receive the gift of the Holy Spirit immediately upon their baptism. Luke now tells us **when** and **how** the gift of the Holy Spirit was given.

Then they laid their hands on them, and they received the Holy Spirit. 8:17

The Holy Spirit was given through the hands of the apostles. Philip could work miracles, but he could not give the miraculous gifts of the Holy Spirit to others. Only the apostles had that power. When the apostles laid their hands on the new converts at Samaria, they were able to prophesy and work miracles. This fulfilled the prophecy of Joel 2:28-32 that Peter quoted and promised on the day of Pentecost. (Acts 2:16-18, 38)

Miraculous gifts were necessary then. They didn't have a New Testament to read. When I was baptized, my father gave me a New Testament and told me to read Ephesians, Philippians and Colossians in order to know how to live the Christian life. These early Christians needed miraculous gifts to instruct them how to live and to prove their teaching was from God. (1 Cor. 12:1-11)

Miraculous gifts cannot be imparted to us today, because all of the apostles are dead. However, we have something better. We have the entire New Testament to read. "That which is perfect" has come! Speaking of the miraculous gifts of the Spirit, Paul wrote, "But whether there be prophecies, they shall fail; whether there be tongues, they shall cease; whether there be knowledge, it shall vanish away. For we know in part, and we prophesy in part. But when that which is **perfect** is come, then that which is in part shall be done away. (1 Cor. 13:8-10) The Greek word translated "perfect" is *teleion*, a neuter adjective meaning "complete, entire, as opposed to what is partial and limited." [20]

When Simon saw that through the laying on of the apostles' hands the Holy Spirit was given, he offered them money, saying, "Give me also this power, that on

---

[20] Wesley J. Perschbacher, *The New Analytical Greek Lexicon*, p. 404

whomsoever I lay hands, he may receive the Holy Spirit." 8:18-19

Simon was in the habit of buying and selling magical tricks. If he had the power of the apostles, he could become rich. Simon was seeking to purchase the gift that God had given only to the apostles. "When Simon saw that through laying on of the apostles' hands the Holy Spirit was given, he offered them money." Some today need to see what Simon saw! Only the apostles had the power to impart the gift of the Holy Spirit. Simon knew he did not have that power, and no one today has that power! Those who claim to have the miraculous gift of the Holy Spirit today need to listen to Peter's rebuke of Simon.

But Peter said to him, "Your money perish with you, because you have thought that the gift of God may be purchased with money. You have neither part nor lot in this matter, for your heart is not right in the sight of God." 8:21

Simon was in a lost condition because his heart was not right. God had given the apostles the power to impart the gift of the Holy Spirit. That power belonged to the apostles. Then Peter told Simon what every fallen Christian must do to be restored to a right relationship with God.

"Repent therefore of this your wickedness and pray God, if perhaps the thought of your heart may be forgiven you. For I perceive that you are in the gall of bitterness and in the bond of iniquity." 8:22-23

Simon was in great bitterness and bound by sin, but he could be forgiven if he would repent and pray to God. The apostle John wrote, "If we confess our sins, he is faithful and just to forgive us our sins, and to cleanse us from all unrighteousness." (1 John 1:9) The joy of our salvation may be restored to us. (Psalm 51:12)

Then Simon answered and said, "Pray to the Lord for me, that none of these things which you have spoken come upon me." And they, when they had testified and preached the word of the Lord, returned to Jerusalem and preached in many villages of the Samaritans. 8:24-25

Simon's response showed his repentance. The apostles, Peter and John, preached the word of the Lord to these new Christians in the city of Samaria and witnessed to the resurrection of Jesus. They also preached the gospel to other Samaritans on their way back to Jerusalem.

An angel of the Lord spoke to Philip, saying, "Arise and go toward the south to the way that goes down from Jerusalem to Gaza, which is desert." 8:26

Christ the King was directing the spread of the good news of his kingdom through angels and the Holy Spirit. The word translated **desert** means "unpopulated." An angel instructed Philip to travel south from Samaria to the road from Jerusalem to Gaza. The angel instructed him to go to the unpopulated part of the road that passed through a mountain ravine a few miles southwest of Jerusalem. The remaining part of the road was well populated. [21]

And he arose and went; and behold, there was an Ethiopian eunuch, a court official of Candace, queen of the Ethiopians, who was in charge of all her treasure; and he had come to Jerusalem to worship. And he was returning and sitting in his chariot, and was reading the prophet Isaiah. NASB **8:27-28**

Ethiopia, also called Cush, was on the southern border of Egypt. The queens who ruled in Ethiopia were given the name Candace. Ethiopia was "the most powerful empire in

---

[21] J. W. McGarvey, *New Commentary on Acts of the Apostles* p. 151

Africa" between 250 BC and AD 200. [22] This Ethiopian eunuch was a man of great responsibility being the treasurer of the Queen. He was either a Jew or a convert to the Jewish faith. His devotion to God is seen in his making such a long trip to worship in Jerusalem and in his reading the Holy Scriptures on his return home.

Then the Spirit said to Philip, "Go near and join yourself to this chariot." And Philip ran to him and heard him read the prophet Isaiah, and said, "Do you understand what you are reading?" And he said, "How can I, except some man should guide me?" And he desired Philip that he would come up and sit with him. 8:29-31

The place of the Scripture which he read was this, "He was led as a sheep to the slaughter, and like a lamb dumb before his shearer, so he opened not his mouth. In his humiliation his judgment was taken away, and who shall declare his generation? For his life is taken from the earth." 8:32-33

And the eunuch answered Philip and said, "I pray you, of whom speaks the prophet this? Of himself or of some other man?" Then Philip opened his mouth and began at the same Scripture and preached to him Jesus. 8:34-35

The Ethiopian was willing to be taught. He was reading Isaiah 53:7-8. He had already read the prophet's question in Isaiah 53:1, *"Who has believed our report?"* Most people would not believe the good news about the Messiah. The prophet had predicted in Isaiah 7:14 that the virgin would bear a son whose name would be Immanuel, meaning God with us. The Messiah would grow up *"as a tender plant and as a root out of dry ground."* (53:2) Jesus was born of the

---

[22] Addison-Wesley, *World History Traditions and New Directions,* p. 301

virgin Mary and grew up in the obscure town of Nazareth in Galilee. *"He has no form or comeliness; and when we shall see him, there is no beauty that we should desire him."* (53:2b) He would look ordinary in his appearance. *"He is despised and rejected of men."* (53:3) Jesus had been rejected by the Jews. *"He has borne our griefs and carried our sorrows."* (53:4) Jesus showed compassion for us. *"He was wounded for our transgressions; he was bruised for our iniquities."* (53:5) He was beaten with rods and scourged, and a crown of thorns pierced his head. *"He was led as a lamb to the slaughter."* (53:7) He is our Passover Lamb, who was sacrificed for us to deliver us from the bondage of sin. (1 Cor. 5:7) *And they made his grave with the wicked and with a rich man in his death."* ᴺᴷᴶⱽ (53:9) The Romans prepared graves for Jesus and the two criminals with him. But when Jesus died, a rich man from Arimathea, named Joseph, went to Pilate and asked for the body of Jesus, and he buried him in his own new tomb. (Matthew 27:57-60)

Then God promised, *"He shall prolong his days, and the pleasure of the LORD shall prosper in his hand."* (53:10) The Messiah would be raised from the dead! Jesus was raised from the dead and appeared to many witnesses. The Holy Spirit came upon the apostles on Pentecost giving them inspiration and miracles to confirm their word. (Acts 2:1-35) Jesus is now on his throne at God's right hand exalted as Lord and Christ. Believers are instructed to repent and be baptized in the name of Jesus Christ for the remission of sins. (Acts 2:36-38)

Now as they went down the road, they came to some water. And the eunuch said, "See, here is water. What hinders me from being baptized?" ᴺᴷᴶⱽ **8:36**

There were many pools along the inhabited part of the road that were suitable for immersion in water.

And Philip said, "If you believe with all your heart, you may." And he answered and said, "I believe that Jesus Christ is the Son of God." 8:37

This was the practice of the early church. Romans 10:9-10 teaches, "If you shall confess with your mouth the Lord Jesus, and shall believe in your heart that God has raised him from the dead, you shall be saved. For with the heart man believes unto righteousness and with the mouth confession is made unto salvation."

And he commanded the chariot to stand still; and they both went down into the water, both Philip and the eunuch, and he baptized him. And when they were come up out of the water, the Spirit caught away Philip, that the eunuch saw him no more; and he went on his way rejoicing. 8:38-39

The baptism of the Ethiopian eunuch is here described as going down into the water and coming up out of the water. The Greek word *Baptismos* means immersion. This is the new birth of water and the Spirit. (John 3:5) It is the beginning of a new life in Christ. (Romans 6:3-4) It is followed by rejoicing in the Lord. (Philippians 4:4)

In the conversion of the Ethiopian treasurer, we can see the importance of one soul being saved. He brought the gospel to Ethiopia, the most powerful nation in Africa at that time. He was a man of influence. "Christianity survived in the rugged hills of present-day Ethiopia." [23]

Philip was found at Azotus; and passing through he preached in all the cities till he came to Caesarea. 8:40

The Spirit sent Philip to other places to share the gospel message. Azotus was a Philistine city north of Gaza. Earlier, it was known as Ashdod, one of the Philistine city-states.

---

[23] Addison-Wesley, *World History Traditions and New Directions*, p. 302

(Zech. 9:6) Philip preached in the cities along the coast of the Mediterranean Sea until he came to Caesarea, which was the residence of the Roman governors of Judea. Paul and his companions spent several days in the home of Philip the evangelist in Caesarea, when they were on their way to Jerusalem after the third missionary journey. (Acts 21:8)

NOTES

The Conversion of Saul
Acts 9:1-31

The transforming power of Christ the King is seen in the conversion of Saul of Tarsus. After Jesus appeared to him on the road to Damascus, the persecutor of Christ and his church became the great apostle Paul, who proclaimed the gospel of Christ. (1 Cor. 15:1-11)

Saul, yet breathing out threats and slaughters against the disciples of the Lord, went to the high priest and desired of him letters to Damascus to the synagogues, that if he found any of the way, whether they were men or women, he might bring them bound to Jerusalem. 9:1-2

Saul was determined to destroy what he thought was a threat to the religion of the true God. But his persecution of Christians in Jerusalem had caused them to go to other cities with their teachings about Jesus. In his zeal for God, he was willing to journey over 140 miles to Damascus in Syria to stamp out Christianity. Damascus had a large Jewish population with several synagogues. The letters would give Saul authority to bring Christian Jews back to Jerusalem for trial. Christianity is called "the way" also in Acts 19:9, 19:23, 22:4, 24:14, and 24:22.

And as he journeyed, he came near Damascus; and suddenly there shined round him a light from heaven. It was "about midday," and the light was "above the brightness of the sun," according to 26:13. **And he fell to the earth and heard a voice saying to him, "Saul, Saul, why are you persecuting me?" And he said, "Who are you, Lord?" And the Lord said, "I am Jesus, whom you are persecuting." And he trembling and astonished said, "Lord, what will you have me to do?" 9:3-6**

Saul was surprised and startled! Who was speaking to him? Recognizing the greatness of the one speaking to him, Saul called him "Lord," meaning "master." He was hearing the voice of Jesus. When Saul persecuted Christians, he was persecuting Jesus, because the church is the body of Christ. (Eph. 1:20-23) Saul believed he was doing God's will, but the more he persecuted the church the farther it spread. Saul now realized how terribly wrong he had been. He had thought that Jesus was a dead imposter. Now he is convinced that Jesus is alive, proving his claims to be the divine Son of God. (Romans 1:1-4) Jesus is Lord and Christ, reigning as King from his throne in heaven. Confessing his faith, Saul wanted to know what the Lord wanted him to do.

And the Lord said to him, "Arise and go into the city, and it shall be told you what you must do." 9:6

Neither Jesus nor an angel ever told anyone what to do to be saved, because "we have this treasure in earthen vessels." (2 Cor. 4:7) Jesus always used one of his disciples to deliver the message of salvation. Paul later wrote, "Though we or an angel from heaven preach any other gospel to you than that which we have preached to you, let him be accursed." (Galatians 1:8)

And the men who journeyed with him stood speechless; hearing a voice, but seeing no man. 9:7

The men with Saul were witnesses to the bright light and to the sound of a voice from heaven. With their help, Saul immediately obeyed the Lord's instructions.

And Saul arose from the earth; and when his eyes were opened, he saw no man. But they led him by the hand, and brought him into Damascus 9:7-8

Those who were with Saul saw the bright light, but only Saul was blinded. The Lord had a reason for blinding his eyes. After healing the man born blind, Jesus said, "For judgment I have come into this world, that those who do not see may see; and that those who see may be made blind." ᴺᴷᴶⱽ (John 9:39) As a Pharisee persecuting Christ and his church, Saul thought he could see clearly, but he was blind and lost spiritually. Jesus was showing him his blindness and his need for spiritual sight. And the one who could heal Saul's blindness would be the one who would tell him the truth.

And he was three days without sight, and neither did eat nor drink. 9:9

This verse proves that Saul was not saved on the road to Damascus, as some teach. He was most miserable. In his blindness, he was feeling so intensely the guilt of his sins that he would not eat or drink for three days. He was not rejoicing like the Ethiopian following his baptism. (Acts 8:39)

And there was a certain disciple at Damascus, named Ananias; and the Lord said to him in a vision, "Ananias." And he said, "Behold I am here, Lord." And the Lord said to him, "Arise and go into the street which is called Straight and inquire in the house of Judas for one called Saul of Tarsus, for behold, he is praying and has seen in a vision a man named Ananias coming in and putting his hands on him that he might receive his sight." 9:10-12

In addition to fasting, Saul was praying for three days. One is not saved by prayer alone. God answered his prayers by giving him a sign.

Ananias answered, "Lord, I have heard by many of this man, how much evil he has done to your saints at Jerusalem; and here he has authority from the chief priests to bind all that call on your name." 9:13-14

Because of Saul's reputation, Ananias was reluctant to see him. And he had heard why Saul had come to Damascus.

But the Lord said to him, "Go your way, for he is a chosen vessel to me, to bear my name before the Gentiles, and kings, and the children of Israel. For I will show him how great things he must suffer for my name's sake." 9:15-16

Why did the Lord appear to Saul? He knew Saul's heart. He knew Saul was a truth seeker. He knew that he had a good conscience (Acts 23:1); he wanted to do right. His zeal for God would be used in preaching the gospel. It pleased God to reveal his Son to Saul that he might preach Christ among the Gentiles. (Galatians 1:15-16)

Why did God choose Saul to be the apostle to the Gentiles? He was well qualified. Saul was from Tarsus, the chief city of Cilicia, which was a rival to Alexandria and Athens as a center of Greek learning. He was taught the Greek language and customs from childhood. Later, he would quote Greek poets to the philosophers in Athens. (Acts 17:28) Saul came from a prominent family, and he was born a Roman citizen. (Acts 22:25-28) He would use his Roman citizenship to appeal to Caesar. (Acts 25:11) His Jewish heritage also was impressive: "Circumcised the eighth day, of the stock of Israel, of the tribe of Benjamin, a Hebrew of the Hebrews." (Phil. 3:5) As a youth, he went to Jerusalem to be taught by the most respected rabbi, Gamaliel. (Acts 22:3) Saul was a leader among the Jews, maybe even a member of the Sanhedrin.

Saul was chosen not only to be the apostle to the Gentiles but also to suffer for the name of Jesus. His willingness to suffer for Christ is one of the great proofs of the resurrection of Jesus from the dead. Why would he be willing to suffer "the loss of all things" to be "found in Christ" if he had not seen Jesus on his way to Damascus to persecute Christians? (Philippians 3:7-10) He also told Christians, "For to you it is given in the behalf of Christ, not only to believe on him, but also to suffer for his sake." (Philippians 1:29)

And Ananias went his way and entered into the house; and putting his hands on him said, "Brother Saul, the Lord, even Jesus, who appeared to you in the way as you came, has sent me that you might receive your sight and be filled with the Holy Spirit. And immediately there fell from his eyes as it had been scales, and he received sight again and arose and was baptized." When he had received meat, he was strengthened. 9:17-19

Ananias put his hands on Saul "that he might receive his sight," according to verse 12. Paul later reported in Acts 22:16, what Ananias said to him: "Arise and be baptized and wash away your sins, calling on the name of the Lord." It appears that Paul then received the baptism of the Holy Spirit. Other converts received the gift of the Holy Spirit when the apostles laid their hands on them. But Paul was "an apostle (not sent from men, nor through the agency of man, but through Jesus Christ." [NASB] (Galatians 1:1) He said "The gospel which was preached by me is not according to man. For I neither received it from man, nor was I taught it, but I received it through a revelation of Jesus Christ." [NASB] (Galatians 1:1, 11-12)

Saul was hungry after his three days of fasting. Now that he had been baptized, he could joyfully eat to regain his physical strength as a new creation in Christ.

Saul was certain days with the disciples who were at Damascus. And immediately he preached Christ in the synagogues that he is the Son of God. But all that heard

him were amazed, and said, "Is not this he that destroyed them who called on this name in Jerusalem and came here for that intent, that he might bring them bound to the chief priests?" 9:19-21**

Seeing Jesus on the road made a great difference! Saul entered the synagogues of Damascus not to bind Christians but to free lost souls from the bondage of sin through the gospel of Christ. What a witness!

But Saul increased all the more in strength, and confounded the Jews who dwelt in Damascus, proving that this Jesus is the Christ. 9:22

This verse spans a period of three years and does not reveal how Saul was strengthened. Paul relates the events after his conversion in Galatians 1:16-18. He said, "I did not immediately confer with flesh and blood, nor did I go up to Jerusalem to those who were apostles before me; but I went to Arabia, and returned to Damascus. Then after three years I went up to Jerusalem to see Peter." NKJV

Paul received the gospel that he preached by "a revelation of Jesus Christ." (Galatians 1:11-12) Paul wrote, "For I *received from the Lord* that which I also delivered to you: that the Lord Jesus on the same night in which he was betrayed took bread." NKJV (1 Cor. 11:23) Roper notes, "Paul's account of Jesus' instituting the Lord's Supper was written down before any of the Gospel Accounts recorded the event." [24] Before his ministry, Paul was with Jesus for about the same length of time as the other apostles. The Jews at Damascus were surprised at his preaching Christ.

Now after many days were past, the Jews plotted to kill him. But the plot became known to Saul. And they watched the gates day and night, to kill him. Then the disciples took him by night and let him down through the

---

[24] David L. Roper, *Truth for Today Commentary, Acts 1-14*, p. 342

wall in a large basket. And when Saul had come to Jerusalem, he tried to join the disciples; but they were all afraid of him, and did not believe that he was a disciple. NKJV **9:23-26**

Saul had been the hunter, and now he had become the hunted. After escaping death at Damascus, he went to Jerusalem. However, the disciples in Jerusalem were afraid of him.

But Barnabas took him, and brought him to the apostles, and declared to them how he had seen the Lord in the way, and that he had spoken to him, and how he had preached boldly at Damascus in the name of Jesus. 9:27

Barnabas was an encourager and an exhorter. This is the beginning of his close relationship with Saul, who would be known as Paul.

And he was with them coming in and going out of Jerusalem. And he spoke boldly in the name of the Lord Jesus and disputed with the Grecians; but they went about to slay him. Which when the brethren knew, they brought him down to Caesarea and sent him forth to Tarsus. 9:29-30

Saul was with the disciples in preaching the gospel both in Jerusalem and the surrounding area. The Grecians, or Hellenists, were the Greek speaking Jews. Saul had been among them when they disputed with Stephen and brought him before the Sanhedrin. (6:9-12; 7:58) He was seeking now to show his former associates the truth about Jesus, but they considered him a deserter of the faith. Saul was in Jerusalem only fifteen days (Gal. 1:18), and then he had to return to his home in Tarsus to save his life. In Acts 22:17-21, Paul tells how Jesus warned him to get out of Jerusalem because the Jews would not receive his testimony. He was reluctant to leave, but the Lord had greater plans for him. He would preach to the Gentiles.

So the church throughout all Judea and Galilee and Samaria enjoyed peace, being built up; and going on in the fear of the Lord and in the comfort of the Holy Spirit, it continued to increase. ᴺᴬˢᴮ **9:31**

The best Greek text has "church" instead of "churches." Roper says, "This reading is an unusual use of the word "church" in Acts. Although a number of congregations existed in the three provinces, Luke saw all the Christians in Palestine as comprising "the church" in that area." [25] The church had survived the first persecution brought against it. There was peace for a time after the conversion of Saul. The church was growing in numbers because Jesus Christ was on the throne, and the Holy Spirit was providing comfort and help through miraculous gifts.

---

[25] David L. Roper, *Truth for Today Commentary, Acts 1-14,* p. 352

The Ministry of Peter
Acts 9:32 – 11:18

Peter Heals at Lydda
Acts 9:32-35

And it came to pass as Peter passed throughout all quarters, he came down also to the saints who lived at Lydda. And there he found a certain man named Aeneas, who had kept to his bed eight years and was paralyzed. And Peter said to him, "Aeneas, Jesus Christ makes you whole: arise and make your bed." And he arose immediately. 9:32-35

Through his apostles, Jesus continued to heal those who were paralyzed. The healing power of the Holy Spirit produced faith in those hearing the gospel of Christ.

Peter Raises the Dead at Joppa
Acts 9:36-43

Now there was at Joppa a certain disciple named Tabitha, which by interpretation is called Dorcas. This woman was full of good works and alms deeds which she did. And it came to pass in those days that she was sick and died. 9:36-37

The disciples sent two men to Lydda, desiring Peter to come to Joppa. **9:38** Peter went with them, and they brought him to the upper chamber, where all the widows were weeping and showing the clothes that Dorcas had made. **9:39 But Peter put them all out, and knelt down, and prayed; and turning to the body said, "Tabitha, arise." And she opened her eyes; and when she saw Peter, she sat up. 9:40** This miracle caused many to believe in the Lord. And Peter stayed in Joppa many days with Simon a tanner. **9:41-43**

Peter Preaches to Gentiles
Acts 10:1 – 11:18

There was a certain man in Caesarea called Cornelius, a centurion of the cohort called the Italian, a devout man, and one who feared God with all his house, who gave much alms to the people and prayed to God always. 10:1-2

Caesarea was the headquarters of Roman governors over Palestine. Herod the Great rebuilt the city and named it in honor of Augustus Caesar. As a centurion, Cornelius was in command of a hundred soldiers. He was part of a cohort that usually consisted of six hundred men.

Although Cornelius was a Gentile, he had come to believe in the true God. He had influenced his household to fear God, and he showed his faith by helping those in need and devoting himself to God in prayer. He was seeking the truth and desired to please God.

He saw clearly in a vision about the ninth hour of the day an angel of God coming in to him and saying to him, "Cornelius." And when he looked on him, he was afraid and said, "What is it, Lord?" And he said to him, "Your prayers and your alms are come up for a memorial before God. And now send men to Joppa and call for one Simon, whose surname is Peter; he lodges with one Simon a tanner, whose house is by the sea side. He shall tell you what you ought to do." And when the angel who spoke to Cornelius was departed, he called two of his household servants and a devout soldier of those that waited on him continually. And when he had declared all these things to them, he sent them to Joppa. 10:3-8

Cornelius saw this vision about three o'clock in the afternoon, the hour of prayer. (Acts 3:1) God hears those who are seeking to please him. (Matthew 7:7) However, the angel did not tell Cornelius what to do to be saved. Instead, he instructed him to send for a man who would tell him what he should do. The gospel treasure is in "earthen vessels." (2 Corinthians 4:5-7) After making known all these things to two servants and a soldier, Cornelius sent them to Joppa for Peter.

The next day as the three men went on their journey and came near to the city of Joppa, Peter went up on the housetop to pray as the noon meal was being prepared. **And he became very hungry. But while they made ready, he fell into a trance and saw heaven opened, and a certain vessel descending to him ... wherein were all manner of four-footed beasts of the earth, and wild animals, and creeping things, and fowls of the air. And there came a voice to him, "Rise, Peter, kill and eat." But Peter said, "Not so, Lord, for I have never eaten anything that was common or unclean."** At first, Peter must have thought this was a test of his faith and devotion to God. **And the voice spoke to him again the second time, "What God has cleansed, do not call common." This was done three times; and the vessel was received up again into heaven." 10:9-16**

While Peter was wondering about the meaning of the vision, the three men sent by Cornelius were at the gate of Simon's house, and they asked whether Peter was there. Then the Spirit said to Peter, **"Behold, three men seek you. Arise therefore, go down and go with them, doubting nothing; for I have sent them." 10:17-20**

The vision had prepared Peter for the Holy Spirit's message. The men explained to Peter why they had come. They said, **"Cornelius the centurion, a just man, and one who fears God and of good report among the nation of the Jews, was warned from God by a holy angel to send** for you into his house and to hear words from you." **10:21-22**

Then Peter invited the men in and gave them lodging for the night. The following day, Peter and some brethren from Joppa went with them to Caesarea, which was thirty miles north of Joppa. **10:23** Peter took with him six Jewish brethren as witnesses. (10:44-46 and 11:12)

As Peter began to enter the house, Cornelius met him and fell down at his feet and worshiped him. But Peter lifting him up said, **"Stand up, I myself also am a man." 10:24-26** He made it clear that he is not to be worshiped.

When Peter entered the house, he found many had come to hear him, because Cornelius had called together his relatives and close friends. And he said to them, **"You know how that it is an unlawful thing for a man that is a Jew to keep company, or come to one of another nation; but God has shown me that I should not call any man common or unclean." 10:27-28**

Roper wrote, "These words were probably spoken as much for the benefit of the six brethren who had come with him as for the sake of the Gentiles who had assembled. Most, if not all, of those present were probably 'God-fearers' like Cornelius and attended synagogue services. They would know both the law and the traditions of the Jews." [26]

Peter then asked, **"For what intent have you sent for me?" 10:29** Although the messengers had told Peter the purpose of his coming, he wanted to hear from Cornelius himself the reason for his sending for him.

And Cornelius said, "Four days ago I was fasting until this hour; and at the ninth hour I prayed in my house. And, behold, a man stood before me in bright clothing and said, 'Cornelius, your prayer is heard, and your alms

---

[26] David L. Roper, *Truth for Today Commentary, Acts 1-14*, p. 397

are had in remembrance in the sight of God. Send therefore to Joppa, and call here Simon, whose surname is Peter; he is lodged in the house of Simon a tanner by the sea side. When he comes, he shall speak to you.' Immediately therefore I sent to you, and you have done well that you are come. Now therefore we are all here present before God to hear all things that are commanded you of God." 10:30-33

We should follow their example when it is time for Bible study and worship. These Gentiles were eager to hear what God wanted them to do. They had not assembled out of duty or to be entertained. They wanted to hear God's word.

Then Peter said, "Of a truth I perceive that God is no respecter of persons. But in every nation, he that fears him and works righteousness is accepted with him." 10:34-36

The Greek word translated "respecter of persons" literally means receiving a face, or judging a person by his looks. Jesus taught us, "Judge not according to the appearance." (John 7:24) The vision of the various birds and animals, followed by the Holy Spirit's instructions, had convinced Peter not to make any difference between Gentiles and Jews. God welcomes those who reverence and obey him, regardless of their race or nationality. He is Lord of all. Man may have peace with his Maker. This good news of peace was made possible by Jesus Christ. It was first preached to the Jews, but it is for all nations. The gospel of Christ brings those of all nations together.

"The word which God sent to the children of Israel, preaching peace by Jesus Christ – He is Lord of all – that word, *I say,* **you know, which was published throughout**

all Judea, and began from Galilee after the baptism which John preached. How God anointed Jesus of Nazareth with the Holy Spirit and with power; who went about doing good and healing all that were oppressed by the devil; for God was with him. And we are witnesses of all things which he did both in the land of the Jews and in Jerusalem; whom they slew and hanged on a tree. Him God raised up the third day and showed him openly; not to all the people, but to witnesses chosen before of God, even to us, who did eat and drink with him after he rose from the dead." 10:37-41

Jesus "went about doing good and healing all that were oppressed by the devil." This is an excellent summary of his life. But surely Peter had much more to say about the life of Jesus. Peter states he was a witness of Jesus being alive after his resurrection from the dead. Jesus ate and drank with his disciples, and he gave them the commission to preach the gospel to all nations.

"And he commanded us to preach to the people and to testify that it is he who was ordained of God to be the Judge of the living and dead." 10:42 The One who died for us will be our Judge on the Judgment Day. (Acts 17:31) **"To him all the prophets give witness that through his name whoever believes in him shall receive the remission of sins." 10:43**

The faith that saves is an obedient faith, for Jesus said, "Not everyone who says to me, 'Lord, Lord,' shall enter into the kingdom of heaven, but he that does the will of my Father who is in heaven." (Matthew 7:21) "He who comes to God must believe that he is and that he is a rewarder of those who diligently seek him." (Heb. 11:6)

While Peter yet spoke these words, the Holy Spirit fell on them all which heard the word. And they of the

circumcision which believed were astonished, as many as came with Peter, because that on the Gentiles also was poured out the gift of the Holy Spirit. For they heard them speak with tongues and magnify God. Then Peter answered, "Can any man forbid water, that these should not be baptized, which have received the Holy Spirit as well as we?" 10:47

The gift of the Holy Spirit was a sign to Jewish brethren who were with Peter that the Gentiles could enter the kingdom by the new birth of water and the Spirit. (John 3:5) On Pentecost, Peter quoted Joel's prophecy, "And it shall come to pass in the last days, says God, **I will pour out of my Spirit upon all flesh.**" (Acts 2:16-17) Obedient believers from all nations would receive the gift. This out pouring of the Spirit's power was also a sign to the Gentiles that Peter's message was from God and that they could be accepted if they would believe.

Peter **commanded them to be baptized in the name of the Lord. Then they prayed him to tarry certain days. 10:48**

The angel had promised Cornelius that Peter would tell him what he should do, and Cornelius had said to Peter, "We are all here present before God to hear all things that are commanded you of God." (10:6, 33) He commanded them to be baptized.

And the apostles and brethren who were in Judea heard that the Gentiles had also received the word of God. And when Peter was come up to Jerusalem, they who were of the circumcision contended with him, saying, "You went in to men uncircumcised and did eat with them." But Peter rehearsed the matter from the beginning. 11:1-4

Peter revealed to them the heavenly vision at Joppa just before the three men from Cornelius came to him. He explained his actions.

"The Spirit told me to go with them, nothing doubting. Moreover, these six brethren accompanied me, and we entered into the man's house. And he showed us how he had seen an angel in his house, which stood and said to him, 'Send men to Joppa, and call for Simon, whose surname is Peter, who shall tell you words whereby you and all your house shall be saved.'" 11:12-14

They were saved by obeying the words of Peter. He commanded them to believe and be baptized. (10:43, 48)

"And as I began to speak, the Holy Spirit fell on them as on us at the beginning. Then I remembered the word of the Lord, how that he said, 'John indeed baptized with water; but you shall be baptized with the Holy Spirit.'" 11:16

The household of Cornelius received the baptism of the Holy Spirit just like the apostles did on the day of Pentecost "at the beginning." No human agency was involved; the power came directly upon them. Peter and the six Jewish brethren with him were "astonished"—they were not expecting it. This proves that the baptism of the Holy Spirit was not a common occurrence in the church. Peter concluded his defense with these words:

"If therefore God gave them the same gift as He gave us when we believed on the Lord Jesus Christ, who was I that I could withstand God?" When they heard these things, they became silent; and they glorified God, saying, "Then God has also granted to the Gentiles repentance to life." NKJV **11:17-18**

The gift of the Holy Spirit was instructive. Jesus had said that the Holy Spirit "will teach you all things." (John 14:26) Because God gave the gift of the Holy Spirit to Cornelius and his household, the apostles understood that the gospel was also for the Gentiles. Peter was given this opportunity to open the door of the kingdom of heaven to the Gentiles as he did to the Jews on Pentecost, because Jesus had given to him "the keys of the kingdom of heaven." (Matthew 16:19) We now have "all things that pertain to life and godliness." (2 Peter 1:3).

NOTES

Power over Persecutors
Acts 11:19 – 12:25

Persecutions caused the gospel of Christ to spread. And Christ the King had power to overcome his persecutors. Saul of Tarsus was converted to the faith; and King Herod was struck down.

Now they who were scattered abroad upon the persecution that arose about Stephen travelled as far as Phoenicia and Cyprus and Antioch, preaching the word to none but to the Jews only. 11:19

Saul's persecution of the church in Jerusalem caused the disciples to flee to the north, taking the gospel with them. (Acts 8:1-4) The kingdom of Christ spread to the Phoenicians; a people located along the Mediterranean coast of northern Palestine. Disciples settled in the cities of Tyre and Sidon. (Acts 15:3; 21:3-7; 27:3) Some went to the island of Cyprus and others to Antioch in Syria. After his conversion, Saul preached in Damascus and in Cilicia around his hometown of Tarsus. (Acts 9:27-30) But at first, the disciples were preaching only to the Jews.

Men from the Mediterranean island of Cyprus and from Cyrene in North Africa came to Antioch, and they spoke to the Grecians, preaching the Lord Jesus. And the hand of the Lord was with them; and a great number believed and turned to the Lord. 11:20-21

The good news that salvation was also for the Gentiles was spreading. Antioch was the third largest city in the world, behind Rome and Alexandria. [27] David Lipscomb wrote, "The hand of the Lord usually means that the miraculous power was exerted. Many of those scattered

---

[27] David L. Roper, *Truth for Today Commentary*, p. 423

abroad had gifts of the Spirit. The exercise of these gifts caused many to believe." [28]

Then the tidings of these things came to the ears of the church which was in Jerusalem; and they sent Barnabas that he should go as far as Antioch. Who, when he came and had seen the grace of God, was glad and exhorted them all that with purpose of heart they would cleave to the Lord. 11:22-23

Barnabas was the ideal man to send because he was an encourager and was from the Greek-speaking island of Cyprus. (Acts 4:36) He exhorted them to remain faithful to the Lord with purpose of heart. Barnabas was **a good man and full of the Holy Spirit and of faith. And much people were added to the Lord. 11:24** David Roper notes, "His emphasis on the *spiritual* growth of the church resulted in the *numerical* growth of the church." [29]

Then Barnabas departed to Tarsus to seek for Saul. 11:25 After Saul's brief visit in Jerusalem, he returned to Tarsus in Cilicia. (Acts 9:26-30) He spent the next seven years in the regions of Syria and Cilicia. (Galatians 1:21) He established churches that he later would visit as he began his second missionary journey, traveling through Syria and Cilicia. (Acts 15:41)

And when he had found him, he brought him to Antioch. So it was that for a whole year they assembled with the church and taught a great many people. 11:26 NKJV

Barnabas and Saul began working together. During this year in Antioch, they were with the church that would send them on their missionary journey. Barnabas made Saul known to the church in Antioch.

---

[28] David Lipscomb, *A Commentary on the Acts of the Apostles,* p. 113
[29] David L. Roper, *Truth for Today Commentary, Acts 1-14,* p, 428

And the disciples were called Christians first in Antioch. 11:26

Isaiah had prophesied, "And the Gentiles shall see your righteousness, and all kings your glory; and you shall be called by a new name, which the mouth of the LORD shall name. (62:2) After Gentiles received God's righteousness, the disciples were called Christians first in the Gentile city of Antioch in Syria. Peter later wrote, "If anyone suffers as a Christian, let him not be ashamed, but let him glorify God in that name." ᴱˢⱽ (1 Peter 4:16)

And in these days, prophets from Jerusalem came to Antioch. And there stood up one of them named Agabus, and signified by the Spirit that there should be a great famine throughout all the world; which came to pass in the days of Claudius Caesar. 11:27-28

Anthony Ash reports evidence that "many parts of the empire experienced crop failures and subsequent food shortages during this period. Judea suffered extreme conditions in AD 46-48. Luke dates the famine by the reign of **Claudius** (AD 41-54)." [30]

Then the disciples, every man according to his ability, determined to send relief to the brethren who dwelt in Judea; which also they did, and sent it to the elders by the hands of Barnabas and Saul. 11:29-30

This shows the confidence that the brethren in Antioch had in Barnabas and Saul. The contribution was sent to the elders, who distributed it to those in need. This is the first time that elders are mentioned in the church. "The leadership of the church was shifting from apostles to elders. The apostleship was a provisional position in the church; the eldership was a permanent position." [31]

---

[30] Anthony Lee Ash, *The Acts of the Apostles, Part I*, p. 166
[31] David L. Roper, *Truth for Today Commentary, Acts 1-14*, p. 434

King Herod Persecutes the Church
Acts 12:1-19

About that time Herod the king stretched forth his hands to vex certain of the church. And he killed James the brother of John with the sword. 12:1-2

Herod Agrippa I was part Idumean (Edomite) and part Jewish. His grandfather was Herod the Great, the king when Jesus was born. His grandmother was Mariamne, a Jewish princess of the Maccabean family. He grew up in the palace at Rome. When Claudius became emperor, he made Agrippa king over all of Palestine, with his palace at Caesarea. Agrippa I was self-indulgent, but he observed Jewish traditions and festivals.

The church had enjoyed peace since the conversion of Saul; but now the king Herod Agrippa was seeking the favor of the Jews. James the brother of John was the first of the apostles to be killed. He had said that he was able to drink the cup that Jesus would drink. (Matthew 20:22) Peter, James and John were part of the inner circle closest to Jesus. They alone witnessed the resurrection of Jairus' daughter and the transfiguration, and they were nearer to him in Gethsemane.

When he saw that this pleased the Jews, he proceeded to seize Peter also. This happened during the Feast of Unleavened bread. After arresting him, he put him in prison, handing him over to be guarded by four squads of four soldiers each. Herod intended to bring him out for public trial after the Passover. NIV 12:3-4

If killing James pleased the Jews, killing Peter would please them even more. Herod and many Jews had come to Jerusalem for the Passover and the Feast of Unleavened Bread. A total of sixteen soldiers were assigned to guard

Peter, four soldiers at a time. Each squad had a three-hour shift during the night. Herod waited until the week of the Passover and Unleavened Bread was over, so he would not offend the Jews by disrupting their holy days.

Peter therefore was kept in prison; but prayer was made without ceasing by the church to God for him. And when Herod would have brought him forth, the same night Peter was sleeping between two soldiers, bound with two chains; and the keepers before the door kept the prison. 12:5-6

Because of his faith, Peter was able to sleep during the night before his trial, although he was chained to two soldiers, one on each side. The other two soldiers guarded the cell door and the prison gate. Peter's escape from prison seemed impossible. But earlier, an angel had delivered him and the other apostles from a prison. (5:19)

And behold, an angel of the Lord stood next to him, and a light shone in the cell. He struck Peter on the side and woke him, saying, "Get up quickly." And the chains fell off his hands. And the angel said to him, "Dress yourself and put on your sandals. And he did so. And he said to him, "Wrap your cloak around you and follow me." And he went out and followed him. He did not know that what was being done by the angel was real, but thought he was seeing a vision. When they passed the first and the second guard, they came to the iron gate leading into the city. It opened for them of its own accord, and they went out and went along one street, and immediately the angel left him. When Peter came to himself, he said, "Now I am sure that the Lord has sent his angel and rescued me from the hand of Herod and from all that the Jewish people were expecting." ESV 12:7-11

This was a miracle!

When he realized this, he went to the house of Mary, the mother of John whose other name was Mark, where many were gathered together and were praying. And when he knocked at the door of the gateway, a servant girl named Rhoda came to answer. Recognizing Peter's voice, in her joy she did not open the gate but ran in and reported that Peter was standing at the gate. They said to her, "You are out of your mind." But she kept insisting that it was so, and they kept saying, "It is his angel." But Peter continued knocking, and when they opened, they saw him and were amazed. ESV **12:12-16**

Their seeing Peter alive was just too good to be true. Are we surprised when our prayers are answered? God can exceed our expectations. (Ephesians 3:20) We are to ask in faith, not doubting (James 1:5); and we should say, "If the Lord wills." (4:14) Perhaps they were resigned to Peter's death and were praying that his faith would not fail him and his suffering would be limited.

After explaining how God had brought him out of the prison, he said, **"Go show these things to James and to the brethren." And he departed, and went to another place. 12:17**

James the Lord's half-brother was a leader in the church in Jerusalem, and Peter wanted to comfort the church. He also needed to find a place to hide.

Now as soon as it was day, there was no small stir among the soldiers ... And when Herod had sought for him and found him not, he examined the keepers and commanded that they should be put to death. And he went down from Judea to Caesarea and abode there. 12:18-19 This was the harsh penalty usually inflicted on a soldier who allowed a prisoner to escape.

Herod's Death
Acts 12:20-25

Now Herod was angry with the people of Tyre and Sidon, and they came to him with one accord, and having persuaded Blastus, the king's chamberlain, they asked for peace, because their country depended on the king's country for food.

On an appointed day Herod put on his royal robes, took his seat upon the throne, and delivered an oration to them. And the people were shouting, "The voice of a god, and not of a man!" Immediately an angel of the Lord struck him down, because he did not give God the glory, and he was eaten by worms and breathed his last. ᴱˢⱽ **12:20-23**

The Jewish first-century historian Josephus tells us that Herod was arrayed in a royal garment made completely of silver, which was illuminated by the reflection of the sun.[32] An angel of God struck him down with a miserable and disgusting illness of worms. Josephus says that Herod suffered for five days before he died. The persecutor was punished!

But the word of God grew and multiplied. And Barnabas and Saul returned from Jerusalem when they had fulfilled their ministry. And they took with them John, whose surname was Mark. 12:24-25

After completing their benevolent work in Jerusalem due to the famine, Barnabas and Saul returned to Antioch with Mark. These three would soon set out together on a missionary journey. (Acts 13:2-5)

---

[32] Josephus, *Antiquities,* 19.8.2

NOTES

The First Missionary Journey
Acts 13 -14

Now there were in the church that was at Antioch certain prophets and teachers. 13:1

Five men are named, beginning with ***Barnabas*** and ending with ***Saul***. The second to be named was ***Simeon called Niger***. Simeon was a common Jewish name; "Niger" is Latin for black. His hair may have been black, and he was given this nickname for the same reason some men are called "Blackie" or "Red" today. ***Lucius of Cyrene*** was probably one of the men from Cyrene who were preaching to the Gentiles in Antioch. (Acts 11:20) ***Manaen*** had been brought up with Herod the tetrarch, who was over Galilee and Perea during Jesus' ministry. This Herod was Antipas, who beheaded John the Baptist.

As they ministered to the Lord and fasted, the Holy Spirit said, "Separate me Barnabas and Saul for the work to which I have called them." 13:2

At the time of his conversion, Saul was informed that he had been chosen to bear witness to the Gentiles. (Acts 26:15-18) As these teachers and prophets led the church in worship, the Holy Spirit spoke through one of them. Barnabas and Saul had been teaching both Jews and Gentiles for a year at Antioch. (Acts 11:25-26) At this time, they were fasting along with the other leaders. Perhaps they were seeking know how they might better serve the Lord.

And when they had fasted and prayed, and laid their hands on them, they sent them away. 13:3

The church at Antioch prepared Barnabas and Saul for their missionary journey to the Gentiles with fasting and prayers. The laying of their hands upon them was not to impart any special power, but to show their blessing and fellowship in the work appointed by God. Saul became the apostle that Jesus Christ had chosen. An apostle is one who is sent on a mission.

They, being sent forth by the Holy Spirit, departed to Seleucia; and from there they sailed to Cyprus. 13:4

Luke emphasizes that the Holy Spirit sent Barnabas and Saul on their missionary journey. Seleucia was the port of Antioch. Seleucus was a Greek army general, who founded the city of Antioch about 300 BC and named its seaport city after himself. Antiochus IV, a king in the Seleucid dynasty, spread the Greek culture from the city of Antioch. He desecrated the temple of God in Jerusalem with pagan idols from May, 168 BC through December, 165 BC. From Antioch, the Holy Spirit is sending his missionaries to the Gentiles to turn them from lifeless idols to serve the living God. From Seleucia, they sailed to the island of Cyprus, the home of Barnabas. (Acts 4:36)

Preaching the Word on Cyprus
Acts 13:5-12

And when they arrived in Salamis, they preached the word of God in the synagogues of the Jews. They also had John as their assistant. 13:5 NKJV

Salamis was the island's eastern port city and the center of commerce. The number of synagogues on the island indicated that there was a large Jewish population. They preached first in the synagogues, giving the Jews the first opportunity to hear the gospel. (Romans 1:16) John Mark was with them as a helper and as an apprentice missionary.

Now when they had gone through the island to Paphos, they found a certain sorcerer, a false prophet, a

Jew whose name was Bar-Jesus, who was with the proconsul, Sergius Paulus, an intelligent man. This man called for Barnabas and Saul and sought to hear the word of God. But Elymas the sorcerer (for so his name is translated) withstood them, seeking to turn the proconsul away from the faith. NKJV **13:6-8**

Paphos, the western seaport, was the capital of Cyprus and the home of Sergius Paulus, the Roman proconsul. The missionaries met a Jewish sorcerer named Bar-Jesus, meaning "Son of Jesus." His given name was "Elymas." He was not claiming to be the son of Jesus Christ. "Jesus" is the Greek form for the Hebrew "Joshua," and it was a common name among the Greek-speaking Jews, as "Joshua" had been earlier. Elymas was an advisor to the proconsul; the Romans were known to seek the advice of soothsayers. However, Sergius Paulus called for Barnabas and Saul to hear the word of God. Fearing that his influence with the proconsul was in jeopardy, Elymas kept interrupting them as they were speaking. **13:8**

Then Saul, who also is called Paul, filled with the Holy Spirit, looked intently at him and said, "O full of deceit and fraud, you son of the devil, you enemy of all righteousness, will you not cease perverting the straight ways of the Lord? And now, indeed, the hand of the Lord is upon you, and you shall be blind, not seeing the sun for a time." And immediately a dark mist fell on him, and he went around seeking someone to lead him by the hand. Then the proconsul believed, when he saw what had been done, being astonished at the teaching of the Lord. NKJV **13:9-12**

From this point forward, Saul is called Paul. His Hebrew name was Saul, but among the Greeks he was known as Paul. Jesus was sending him to the Gentiles. Paul was "filled with the Holy Spirit." The Spirit put these words in Paul's mouth, and the Spirit struck Elymas with blindness for a season. His loss of sight was not just a coincidence; his sight would be restored. The blindness being temporary would prove that this was a miracle from God. Paul and Barnabas knew that the Lord was with them in their mission work. Sergius Paulus believed. He was not only amazed at the miracle but also at the teaching of the Lord Jesus Christ. A Roman proconsul became a Christian. The missionaries were greatly encouraged by the Lord.

Now when Paul and his company loosed from Paphos, they came to Perga in Pamphylia. And John departing from them returned to Jerusalem. 13:13

Paul is mentioned first for the first time; he is now the leader. From Paphos they sailed north to the coast of Asia Minor. They went seven miles up a river to Perga, the capital of Pamphylia. At this time, John Mark left them and went back to Jerusalem. Paul was disappointed by his decision. (Acts 15:38, 39)

Antioch in Pisidia
Acts 13:14-52

But when they departed from Perga, they came to Antioch in Pisidia, and went into the synagogue on the Sabbath and sat down. After the reading of the law and the prophets, the rulers of the synagogue sent to them, saying, "You men and brethren, if you have any word of exhortation for the people, say on." 13:14-15

Antioch of Pisidia was the chief city in the Roman province of Galatia. Paul wrote in Galatians 4:13, "You know how through infirmity of the flesh I preached the gospel to you at first." The area around Perga is marshland and mosquitos infested. It is suggested that Paul became sick with malaria on the way to Antioch. They had to hike a mountain path through forests with wild beasts and bandits before arriving at Antioch of Pisidia. (cf. 2 Corinthians 11:26) Paul and Barnabas entered the synagogue on the Sabbath, where they were invited to speak. The rulers of the synagogue may have heard that Paul had studied under the famous rabbi Gamaliel.

And Paul stood up, and motioning with his hand, he said, "Men of Israel, and you who fear God, listen: The God of this people Israel chose our fathers, and made the people great during their stay in the land of Egypt, and with an uplifted arm He led them out from it. And for a period of about forty years, He put up with them in the wilderness. And when He had destroyed seven nations in the land of Canaan, He distributed their land as an inheritance—*all of which took* about four hundred and fifty years. After these things He gave *them* judges until Samuel the prophet." NASB **13:16-20**

Jews and God-fearing Gentiles were in the audience, and Paul wanted them to pay attention to his message that would show that God had chosen Israel to bring the Christ into the world for the salvation of all nations. With great power, God brought the people of Israel out of Egypt and gave them the land of Canaan as an inheritance. Paul said that their time in Egypt, the wilderness wanderings and the conquest of Canaan was a period of about four hundred and fifty years. And after these things, God gave to them judges until Samuel. (The KJV incorrectly applies the four hundred years to the period of the judges.)

"And afterward they desired a king; and God gave to them Saul the son of Kish, a man of the tribe of Benjamin, by the space of forty years. And when he had removed him, he raised up unto them David to be their

king, to whom also he gave testimony and said, 'I have found David the son of Jesse, a man after my own heart, who shall fulfill all my will.' Of this man's seed God has according to his promise raised to Israel a Savior, Jesus." 13:21-23

When the people asked for a king, God made Saul king of Israel. (1 Samuel 8:5-9) But he was removed because of his disobedience. God then made David king, saying that David was a man after his own heart, who would fulfill his will. God promised to establish the throne of David's seed forever. (2 Samuel 7:12-13) Jesus fulfills this promise. This is the theme of Paul's message.

"Before his coming, John had proclaimed a baptism of repentance to all the people of Israel." And as John was finishing his course, he said, 'What do you suppose I am? I am not he. No, but behold, after me one is coming, the sandals of whose feet I am not worthy to untie.' Brothers, sons of the family of Abraham, and those among you who fear God, to us has been sent the message of this salvation." ESV **13:24-26** John the Baptist had testified concerning Jesus. Now that the King has come, salvation has come!

"For they that dwell at Jerusalem, and their rulers, because they knew him not, nor yet the voices of the prophets which are read every sabbath day, they have fulfilled them in condemning him." 13:27

Because those in Jerusalem and their rulers did not know the prophets, they fulfilled their prophecies by condemning Jesus. Roper notes, "Paul probably paused at this point to quote several prophecies concerning the suffering and death of the Messiah—such passages as Isaiah 53 and Psalm 22.

Instead of *disqualifying* Jesus, His death on the cross *qualified* Him to be the Messiah." [33]

"And though they found no cause of death in Him, they asked Pilate that He should be put to death. Now when they had fulfilled all that was written concerning Him, they took Him down from the tree, and laid Him in a tomb. But God raised Him from the dead. He was seen for many days by those who came up with Him from Galilee to Jerusalem, who are His witnesses to the people. NKJV **13:28-**31

The resurrection of Jesus from the dead proved all that he claimed to be. He was not guilty of blasphemy; he is the Son of God! He is the Savior of the world! He fulfilled all the prophecies concerning the Messiah. (Luke 24:44-47)

"And we declare glad tidings to you, how that the promise which was made to the fathers, God has fulfilled the same to us their children in that he has raised Jesus up again; as it is written in the second Psalm, 'You are my Son, this day have I begotten you.'" 13:32-33

The promise made to Abraham, Isaac and Jacob was, *"In your seed shall all the nations of the earth be blessed."* (Genesis 22:18; 26:4; 28:14) Jesus is the **seed**, who blesses all nations. (Galatians 3:16; 4:4)

"And that He raised Him from the dead, no more to return to corruption, He has spoken thus: *'I will give you the sure mercies of David.'"* NKJV **13:34**

Paul quotes Isaiah 55:3, which promises the forgiveness of sins in the "everlasting covenant" of the Christ. The proof of these blessings is the resurrection of Jesus from the dead. God has made Jesus, who was crucified, both Lord and Christ (Acts 2:30-36) He is now reigning as King over an eternal kingdom.

---

[33] David L. Roper, *Truth for Today Commentary, Acts 1-14*, p. 490

"He says also in another Psalm, 'You shall not suffer your Holy One to see corruption.' For David, after he had served his own generation by the will of God, fell asleep, and was laid to his fathers, and saw corruption. But he, whom God raised up again, saw no corruption." **13:35-37**

Paul is quoting Psalm 16:10, as did Peter on Pentecost. Jesus fulfilled the promise made to the fathers and the prophecies made by the prophets.

"Be it known to you therefore, men and brethren, that through this man the forgiveness of sins is preached to you. And by him all that believe are justified from all things, from which you could not be justified by the law of Moses." **13:38-39**

The promise to the fathers was, "In your seed shall all the nations of the earth be blessed." (Gen. 22:18) The seed is Jesus Christ and the blessing is the forgiveness of sins. Paul had quoted God's testimony that David was a man after God's own heart in verse 22. David was not sinless. In fact, David committed two sins that were punishable by death under the law of Moses. But God showed David mercy and forgave him, when he repented with "a broken and contrite heart." (Read Psalm 51 and Psalm 32, which is quoted in Romans 4:5-8 to explain how we are now justified. See Isaiah 55:6-9)

"Beware therefore, lest that come upon you which is spoken of in the prophets. 'Behold, you despisers, marvel and perish! For I work a work in your days, a work which you will by no means believe, though one were to declare it to you.'" NKJV **13:40-41**

Habakkuk 1:5 is quoted that predicted the destruction of Judah by the Chaldeans in 586 BC. God is merciful to believers who repent, but he will judge the wicked.

As they went out, the people begged that these things might be told them the next Sabbath. After the meeting of the synagogue broke up, many Jews and devout converts to Judaism followed Paul and Barnabas, who, as they spoke with them, urged them to continue in the grace of God. 13:42-43 ᴱˢⱽ They were wanting them to continue investigating God's message.

The next Sabbath almost the whole city gathered to hear the word of the Lord. But when the Jews saw the crowds, they were filled with jealousy and began to contradict what was spoken by Paul, reviling him. And Paul and Barnabas spoke out boldly, saying, "It was necessary that the word of God be spoken first to you. Since you thrust it aside and judge yourselves unworthy of eternal life, behold, we are turning to the Gentiles. For so the Lord has commanded us, saying, *'I have made you a light for the Gentiles, that you may bring salvation to the ends of the earth.'"* ** ᴱˢⱽ **13:44-47

The gospel was to be preached to the Jews first, because they were expecting the Messiah. Unbelievers judge themselves unworthy of eternal life. Paul was given a special mission to the Gentiles. (26:16-18)

And when the Gentiles heard this, they were glad and glorified the word of the Lord; and as many as were ordained to eternal life believed. 13:48

The Greek word may be translated 'ordained" ᴷᴶⱽ or 'appointed.' ᴺᴷᴶⱽ, ᴺᴬˢᴮ, ᴺᴵⱽ Those who are appointed to eternal life are believers. Roper says, "This phrase could even be translated, 'as many as believed were appointed to eternal life.' The Jews were jealous, but the Gentiles were joyous. The Jews opposed the Word, while the Gentiles glorified the word. The Jews judged themselves unworthy, but the Gentiles were 'appointed to eternal life.'" [34]

And the word of the Lord was being spread throughout all the region. But the Jews stirred up the devout and prominent women and the chief men of the city, raised up persecution against Paul and Barnabas, and expelled them from their region. But they shook off the dust from their feet against them, and came to Iconium. NKJV **13:49-51**

The shaking of dust off one's feet was a Jewish custom signifying that a place or a person had rejected God's word and was unclean.

And the disciples were filled with joy and with the Holy Spirit. 13:52

It was Paul's practice as an apostle to lay his hands on believers to impart miraculous gifts of the Holy Spirit. The new church leaders at Antioch in Pisidia needed inspired knowledge and wisdom for the church to grow in the faith, and they needed signs to confirm their word.

Iconium in Galatia
Acts 14:1-4

Now it happened in Iconium that they went to the synagogue of the Jews, and so spoke that a great multitude both of the Jews and also of the Greeks believed. NKJV **14:1**

The city of Iconium was over eighty miles southeast of Antioch. Located where several Roman roads met, Iconium was the most important city of that area. Therefore, it was an ideal center for missionary work. The gospel of Christ was well received by a large number of Jews and Greek-speaking Gentiles.

---

[34] David L. Roper, *Truth for Today Commentary, Acts 1-14*, p, 498

The First Missionary Journey | 103

But the unbelieving Jews stirred up the Gentiles ... against the brethren. 14:2

Opposition again came from Jews who rejected their message. The Greek word that is translated "unbelieving" literally means "disobeying." A literal translation of verse two is: "But the Jews *that were disobedient* stirred up the souls of the Gentiles." ASV

Instead of leaving because of opposition, Paul and Barnabas stayed **a long time** in Iconium, **speaking boldly in the Lord, who gave testimony to the word of his grace, and granted signs and wonders to be done by their hands. 14:3**

Once again, we see the Holy Spirit at work in the early church. He was inspiring the preaching of the gospel and was confirming their messages with miracles. They were probably several months in Iconium.

But the multitude of the city was divided; and part held with the Jews, and part with the apostles. 14:4

When the truth is taught, some will believe and some will not. Jesus said, "I came not to send peace, but a sword, for I am come to set a man at variance against his father." (Matthew 10:34-35) Upon hearing the gospel of Christ, the city of Iconium was divided. Both Paul and Barnabas are called "apostles" in verses 4 and 14. Paul had been called by Christ to be an apostle to the Gentiles, and he was an apostle like Peter. (Galatians 2:7-8) Wade observes, "Barnabas, on the other hand, had no special call and did not meet the qualifications of the original Twelve. In what sense, then, was he an apostle? Apparently, the term is used here in the more general sense of 'one who is sent.'" [35] Barnabas had been sent on this mission trip.

---

[35] John W. Wade, *Acts*, p. 146

And when an attempt was made by both the Gentiles and the Jews with their rulers, to mistreat and to stone them, they became aware of it and fled to the cities of Lycaonia, Lystra and Derbe." 14:5-6 NASB**

Jesus had said, "When they persecute you in this city, flee into another." (Matthew 10:23) Lycaonia was a district in Galatia.

And there they preached the gospel. And there sat a certain man at Lystra, impotent in his feet, being a cripple from his mother's womb, who never had walked. This man heard Paul speak, who, steadfastly beholding him and perceiving that he had faith to be healed, said with a loud voice, "Stand upright on your feet." And he leaped and walked. 14:7-10

This miracle was like Peter's healing the lame man at the temple in Acts 3. Although both men had been lamed from birth and had never walked, they were healed instantly; they immediately leaped and walked. However, there were differences. The cripple healed at the temple was not expecting to be healed; Peter "took him by the right hand and lifted him up." (Acts 3:7) Paul perceived that the cripple at Lystra "had faith to be healed," so when he told him to stand up, he had faith to stand up without Paul's aid. In his preaching, Paul surely spoke of miracles performed by Jesus and his apostles. The word of God, which relates these miracles, produces faith. (Romans 10:17, John 20:30-31)

And when the people saw what Paul had done, they lifted up their voices, saying in the speech of Lycaonia, "The gods are come down to us in the likeness of men." 14:11

The people of Lystra believed an old legend that at one time Zeus and Hermes had visited their city disguised as men. Seeking hospitality, they were rejected by the people of the city. Only a poor couple entertained them, not realizing they were deities. Since they had served the gods unknowingly, they were rewarded and everyone else punished.[36] The people of Lystra were superstitious and did not want to make the same mistake again, especially because Lystra's patron god was Zeus.

Barnabas they called Zeus, and Paul they called Hermes because he was the chief speaker. The priest of Zeus, whose temple was just outside the city, brought bulls and wreaths to the city gates because he and the crowd wanted to offer sacrifices to them. 14:12-13 NIV

The Greek text has "Zeus" and "Hermes." The KJV has "Jupiter" and "Mercury" — the names the Romans gave to these gods. Lystra worshiped the Greek gods. The bulls to be sacrificed were decorated with colorful wreaths of flowers placed around their necks. The people were planning a great feast with Barnabas and Paul as their honored guests.

But when the apostles Barnabas and Paul heard of this, they tore their clothes and rushed out into the crowd, shouting: "Men, why are you doing this? We too are only men, humans like you. We are bringing you good news, telling you to turn from these worthless things to the living God, who made heaven and earth and sea and everything in them. In the past, he let all nations go their own way. Yet he has not left himself without testimony: He has shown kindness by giving you rain from heaven and crops in their seasons; he provides you with plenty of food and fills your hearts with joy." NIV **14:14-17**

Barnabas is mentioned first, because the people thought he was their chief god Zeus; the attention of the people would have been upon Barnabas. He and Paul tore their

---

[36] David L. Roper, *Truth for Today Commentary, Acts 1-14,* p. 516

clothes to show their extreme displeasure and distress at the thought of being worshiped as gods. They mingled among the people to prove that they were mere men. They were only the spokesmen for the all-powerful God, who had made the lame man walk. Paul told the people to turn from their idols to the living God who created heaven and earth and everything in them. He is the One who gives us rain and fruitful seasons as a witness to his goodness.

Even with these words, they had difficulty keeping the crowd from sacrificing to them. NIV **14:18**

Paul and Barnabas must have disappointed the crowd; there would be no celebration, no feast. They had humiliated the priest of Zeus, by exposing the uselessness of his sacrifices. Paul and Barnabas did not give the people what they wanted. Modern day "experts on church growth" tell us to find out what the people want and then give it to them. There could have been a mega church at Lystra if Paul and Barnabas had only done that, but it would not have been the Lord's church.

And there came certain Jews from Antioch and Iconium, who persuaded the people, and having stoned Paul, dragged him out of the city, supposing he had been dead. 14:19

Just as Saul of Tarsus had traveled over 100 miles to persecute Christians in Damascus, now zealous Jews from Antioch and Iconium were willing to go over 100 miles to kill him. They were able to persuade the superstitious people of Lystra that Paul had healed the lame man by the power of evil spirits. The Jews had accused Jesus of having "a devil." (John 8:48) To think that evil spirits had come to Lystra terrified them. So, they listened to these Jews. Paul may have been preaching in the marketplace, when they began throwing stones at him until he was unconscious. Then they dragged his bloody body over the rough pavement and through a field away from the city and left him for dead. Paul later writes of his being stoned (2 Cor. 11:25) and his being "caught up into paradise." (2 Cor. 12:1-4)

As the disciples stood around him (14:20), they were overcome with grief. A young man named Timothy was among the new converts at Lystra. (Acts 16:1) Paul called him "a beloved son" in 2 Timothy 1:2, indicating he had converted him. Paul wrote to Timothy, "But you followed my teaching, conduct, purpose, faith, patience, love, perseverance, persecutions, sufferings, such as happened to me at Antioch, at Iconium and at Lystra; what persecutions I endured, and out of them all the Lord delivered me!" NASB (2 Timothy 3:10-11) The experience of witnessing these things would surely leave a lasting impression upon Timothy. Paul later had this to say about Timothy, "I have no man likeminded, who will naturally care for you." (Philippians 2:20) Also among the converts were Timothy's grandmother Lois and his mother Eunice.

However, ... he rose up and went into the city. And the next day he departed with Barnabas to Derbe. NKJV **14:20**

As the disciples no doubt were making plans for his burial, Paul opened his eyes and got up. He courageously entered the city where they had stoned him. Paul later wrote to Timothy, "God has not given us the spirit of fear; but of power, and of love, and of a sound mind. Therefore, be not ashamed of the testimony of our Lord, nor of me his prisoner; but be a partaker of the afflictions of the gospel according to the power of God." (2 Tim 1:7)

Timothy had seen Paul living by these words; Paul had given to Timothy and to us a good example to follow. The next day Paul and Barnabas left for Derbe. This would be a trip of about sixty miles to the southeast.[37] Paul was healed completely with no lingering after-effects. Imagine a person being stoned today, and dragged through a city, and left for dead in a field; how many days would that person need to spend in a hospital? Yes, it was a miracle!

The results at Derbe were rewarding. They **preached the gospel to that city and made many disciples.** NKJV **14:21** There was no persecution or opposition at Derbe. Gaius of Derbe was one of Paul's traveling companions to Jerusalem at the end of the third missionary journey. (Acts 20:4) Where would Paul and Barnabas go from Derbe? Paul was not far now from his home in Tarsus, and soon they could be in Syrian Antioch with an opportunity to rest from their hardships. But their new converts need to be encouraged and strengthened. They needed to be organized as churches with leaders.

They returned again to Lystra, and to Iconium and to Antioch, confirming the souls of the disciples, and exhorting them to continue in the faith, and that we must through much tribulation enter into the kingdom of God. 14:21-22

Christians should remain faithful when persecuted, because we enter the heavenly kingdom of God "through much tribulation." Jesus told us, "In the world you shall have tribulation." (John 16:33) The saved in heaven will have come "out of great tribulation." (Rev. 7:9-15) Paul serves as an example. (Galatians 6:17)

---

[37] John W. Wade, *Acts,* p. 151

And when they had ordained elders in every church and had prayed with fasting, they commended them to the Lord, on whom they believed. 14:23

In each congregation, a plural number of elders were appointed to oversee the work. There must have been mature, spiritually-minded men who had been either Jewish leaders or God-fearing Gentiles like Cornelius. The qualifications of elders, also called bishops, are given in 1 Timothy 3:1-7. Paul laid his hands on new converts for them to receive gifts of the Holy Spirit. (Acts 19:1-7) These churches would have inspired men with the gifts of wisdom, knowledge, and prophecy. (1 Corinthians 12:7-11; Galatians 3:5) The importance of their work was seen by their praying and fasting.

Paul and Barnabas completed their missionary journey by appointing elders in all the congregations that they had established in the Roman province of Galatia. (14:23) Paul's letter to the Galatians is to these churches.

And after they had passed through Pisidia, they came to Pamphylia. And when they had preached the word in Perga, they went down to Attalia. And from there they sailed to Antioch, from where they had been recommended to the grace of God for the work which they fulfilled. 14:24-26

They had not preached at Perga before, but this time they did. Then they went to Attalia on the coast and found a ship going to Antioch, where they had been sent on the missionary journey that they had now completed.

And when they were come and had gathered the church together, they reported all that God had done with them, and how he had opened the door of faith to the Gentiles. And there they stayed a long time with the disciples. 14:27-28

Honor and praise belong to the Lord for the work he does through us. The Holy Spirit was working through the church! Given an opportunity, Gentiles entered the door of faith! Paul and Barnabas probably stayed at least a year at Antioch, as before. (11:25-26)

The Meeting at Jerusalem
Acts 15

Certain men who came down from Judea taught the brethren and said, "Except you are circumcised after the manner of Moses, you cannot be saved." 15:1

These Jewish brethren from Judea taught that one had to become a proselyte Jew by circumcision in order to receive God's blessing of salvation. They believed that the large number of Gentile Christians in Antioch and elsewhere were not fully converted.

When therefore Paul and Barnabas had no small dissension and disputation with them, they determined that Paul and Barnabas, and certain other of them, should go up to Jerusalem to the apostles and elders about this question. 15:2

Referring to these Judaizing teachers, Paul later wrote, "To whom we gave place by subjection, no, not for an hour; that the truth of the gospel might continue with you." (Galatians 2:5) The Holy Spirit had revealed that they should make this trip to Jerusalem, because Paul said, "I went up by revelation." (Galatians 2:2) Among those that went with Paul and Barnabas to Jerusalem was Titus, a Gentile convert. (Galatians 2:1)

On their way to Jerusalem, **they passed through Phoenicia and Samaria, declaring the conversion of the Gentiles; and they caused great joy to all the brethren. 15:3** These congregations had some Gentile members, and they rejoiced upon hearing of this report.

And when they were come to Jerusalem, they were received of the church and of the apostles and elders, and

they declared all things that God had done with them. But there rose up certain of the sect of the Pharisees which believed, saying, "It was needful to circumcise them and to command them to keep the law of Moses." 15:4-5

God had shown his acceptance of the Gentiles who were converted by his miraculous confirmations of the Holy Spirit. The church, for the most part, welcomed Paul and Barnabas. Christians who had been Pharisees were not giving up their old ways of thinking. Paul was able to understand their feelings; he had been a strict Pharisee. But when he was converted to Christ, Paul was led to see that Christianity was much more than just adding faith in Jesus Christ to the doctrines he had held as a Pharisee. He now recognized that man is not justified by works of the law but by grace through faith in Jesus. These Jewish Christians failed to understand that the new covenant of Christ had replaced the covenant of Moses. Many today have the same problem; they go back to the law of Moses to justify their religious practices.

And the apostles and elders came together for to consider this matter. 15:6

Before the whole assembly, Paul and Barnabas reported their work among the Gentiles. When some spoke up and demanded that the Gentiles should be circumcised, the leaders of the church met privately with Paul and Barnabas. (Galatians 2:2) After discussing the issues with them, these men found that they were in agreement. Then James and Peter and John gave the right hand of fellowship to Paul and Barnabas, according to Galatians 2:9. At this time, Paul reports, "Not even Titus who was with me, being a Greek, was compelled to be circumcised." NKJV (Galatians 2:3) Then the apostles and the elders returned with Paul and Barnabas to the general assembly. They would address the meeting with speakers.

And when there had been much disputing, Peter rose up and said to them, "Men and brethren you know how that a good while ago God made choice among us, that the Gentiles by my mouth should hear the word of the gospel and believe. And God, who knows the hearts, bore them witness, giving them the Holy Spirit, even as he did to us; and put no difference between us and them, purifying their hearts by faith. Now therefore why do you tempt God, to put a yoke upon the neck of the disciples, which neither our fathers nor we were able to bear? But we believe that through the grace of the Lord Jesus Christ we shall be saved, even as they." 15:7-11

The outpouring of the Holy Spirit's power upon the household of Cornelius (Acts 10:44-48) served as God's witness that the Gentiles would be accepted by God without circumcision. The same salvation is for both Jews and Gentiles, because our hearts are not purified by the works of the law, but by God's grace through faith in Jesus Christ.

All the multitude kept silence, and gave audience to Barnabas and Paul, declaring what miracles and wonders God had done among the Gentiles by them. 15:12

Barnabas was respected in Jerusalem, and he may have spoken first on this occasion. Their work among the Gentiles was confirmed by God "bearing them witness, both by signs and wonders, and with various miracles, and gifts of the Holy Spirit." (Hebrews 2:3-4)

After they finished speaking, James replied, "Brothers, listen to me. Simeon has related how God first visited the Gentiles, to take from them a people for his name. And with this the words of the prophets agree, just as it is written,

> *'After this I will return,*
> *and build again the tent of David that has fallen;*
> *and I will rebuild its ruins,*
>   *and I will restore it;*
> *that the remnant of mankind may seek the Lord,*
> *and all the Gentiles, who are called by my name,*
>   *says the Lord, who makes these things known*
> *from of old.'"* ᴱˢⱽ **15:13-18**

The third speech was by James, the half-brother of Jesus. (Matt. 13:55; 1 Cor. 15:5-7) James, the apostle and brother of John, had been killed by Herod. (Acts 12:2) This James was a leader in the church in Jerusalem. (Gal. 2:9) James called upon his audience to pay close attention to his words. He reminded them of what Peter (Simeon) had just related. God had visited the Gentiles to take out of them a people for his name. God did not require them to be circumcised, but to be baptized. (Acts 10:47-48) Then James quoted the prophecy of Amos 9:11-12, which predicted that when David's house was restored, the Gentiles who were seeking the Lord would be a people, called by his name. (2 Sam. 7:11b-13)

> **"Therefore my judgment is that we should not trouble those of the Gentiles who turn to God, but should write to them to abstain from things polluted by idols, and from sexual immorality, and from what has been strangled and from blood. For from ancient generations Moses has had in every city those who proclaim him, for he is read every Sabbath in the synagogues."** ᴱˢⱽ **15:19-21**

James was not alone in this judgment, for the leaders of the church in their private meeting had come to this agreement, being guided by the Holy Spirit. (15:6, 28) When they returned to the public meeting, they had a plan for Peter to speak first, followed by Barnabas and Paul, and then

James was to present their conclusion. They had agreed not to trouble the Gentile converts. God-fearing Gentiles had attended the Jewish synagogues every Sabbath and were aware that God wants his people to abstain from things polluted by idols, from sexual immorality, from things strangled and from blood. Moses defined these sins, explaining why they were wrong and sinful. But all these prohibitions had been bound on the Gentiles by the time of the Flood. (Genesis 1:27-28; Genesis 2:24; Genesis 9:4)

Then it pleased the apostles and elders, with the whole church, to send chosen men of their own company to Antioch with Paul and Barnabas, namely, Judas surnamed Barsabas and Silas, chief men among the brethren." 15:22

They agreed to send a letter to the church in Antioch with Judas Barsabas and Silas, who were prophets in the church at Jerusalem. **15:32** We are introduced to Silas, who would be Paul's traveling companion on his second missionary journey. The church in Jerusalem wrote the follower letter:

"The apostles and elders and brethren send greetings to the brethren which are of the Gentiles in Antioch and Syria and Cilicia:" 15:23

The letter begins by recognizing the Gentiles as brethren. The greeting also indicates that Judaizing teachers were not only in Antioch but also throughout Syria and as far west as Cilicia. On his second missionary journey, Paul delivered copies of this letter to the churches in Phrygia and Galatia. (Acts 16:4-6) These churches would include Derbe, Lystra, Iconium, and Antioch of Pisidia. These false teachers were a major problem in the first century. Galatians was written to combat this heresy.

"Since we have heard that some of our number to whom we gave no instruction have disturbed you with *their* words, unsettling your souls, it seemed good to us, having become of one mind, to select men to send to you with our beloved Barnabas and Paul, men who have risked their lives for the name of our Lord Jesus Christ. Therefore we have sent Judas and Silas, who themselves will also report the same things by word of mouth. For it seemed good to the Holy Spirit and to us to lay upon you no greater burden than these essentials: that you abstain from things sacrificed to idols and from blood and from things strangled and from fornication; if you keep yourselves free from such things, you will do well. Farewell." NASB **15:24-29**

The Judaizers had not been authorized or sent by the church at Jerusalem. The greatest temptations for Gentile Christians would be to eat meats that had been sacrificed to idols, to drink blood, to eat bloody meat and to engage in sexual immorality. Notice, this decision "seemed good to the Holy Spirit." This was an inspired decision. God does not require Gentiles to be circumcised and keep the Law of Moses.

So, when they were dismissed, they came to Antioch; and when they had gathered the multitude together, they delivered the letter, which when they had read, they rejoiced for the consolation. And Judas and Silas, being prophets also themselves, exhorted the brethren with many words, and confirmed them. And after they had tarried there a space, they were let go in peace from the brethren unto the apostles. 15:30-33

Following God's guidance brings comfort, joy, and peace. Judas and Silas confirmed their understanding of the new covenant and strengthened the relationship between Gentile and Jewish Christians. The Judaizing teachers probably left

Antioch at this time, but we find them causing trouble in other places.

The most ancient manuscripts do not have verse 34 that is in the King James Version, and most translations omitted it. Gareth Reece notes, "Many commentators feel that Judas and Silas both returned to Jerusalem to give an account to the church there, but that Silas soon returned to Antioch, where he and Paul soon became fellow workers." [38]

But Paul and Barnabas remained in Antioch, where they and many others taught and preached the word of the Lord. NIV **15:35**

At this time, Paul probably wrote his letter to the Galatians, which includes his rebuke of Peter for his inconsistent association with Gentile brethren at Antioch. (Galatians 2:11-16)

And after some days Paul said to Barnabas, "Let us go again and visit our brethren in every city where we have preached the word of the Lord, and see how they do." 15:37

Paul was eager to learn how they had responded to his letter (Galatians) exposing the Judaizing teachers, who were perverting the gospel of Christ. (Galatians 1:6-7) Barnabas was determined to take John Mark, but Paul did not think Mark was trustworthy.

And there arose a sharp disagreement, so that they separated from each other. Barnabas took Mark with him and sailed away to Cyprus, but Paul chose Silas and departed, having been commended by the brothers to the grace of the Lord. And he went through Syria and Cilicia, strengthening the churches. ESV **15:38-41**

---

[38] Gareth L. Reese, *New Testament History – Acts,* p. 558

However, this disagreement worked out for the furtherance of the gospel. The churches on the island of Cyprus needed strengthening as well as those in Galatia. Also, Barnabas was able to train Mark to become a useful minister. (2 Timothy 4:11) Paul with the prophet Silas would begin his second missionary journey that would take the gospel into Europe.

The Second Missionary Journey
Acts 16

Derbe to Philippi

With Silas as his co-worker, Paul's second missionary journey began with their going through Syria and Cilicia, strengthening the churches (15:41)

Paul came to Derbe and to Lystra. A disciple was there, named Timothy, the son of a Jewish woman who was a believer, but his father was a Greek. He was well spoken of by the brothers at Lystra and Iconium. Paul wanted Timothy to accompany him, and he took him and circumcised him because of the Jews who were in those places, for they all knew that his father was a Greek. ESV **16:1-3**

Derbe was the last place where a church was established on the first journey. Traveling westward, Paul and Silas came into Lystra, the city where Paul had been stoned and left for dead. (Acts 14:8-19) Lystra was the hometown of Timothy, who would become one of Paul's closest co-workers. Paul calls him, "my own son in the faith" (1 Tim. 1:2). Timothy may have already become a teacher, because the brethren in Lystra and Iconium were speaking well of him. Paul writes in 2 Timothy 2:5 of Timothy's "unfeigned faith" which dwelt first in his grandmother Lois and in his mother Eunice. Timothy and his mother and grandmother likely became Christians during Paul's first visit to Lystra.

Consider the following comments by David Roper about Timothy's family: "Eunice was married to a Gentile husband; Timothy's **father was a Greek**. Since marriages were normally arranged in those days, we assume this was not

Eunice's decision, but that of her father. Because Timothy's grandfather is not held up by Paul as a good influence on young Timothy, it can be assumed that he arranged the marriage to a Gentile for financial reasons. Eunice's husband did not share her faith and probably actively opposed the practice of her religion. Since Lois and Eunice are pictured by Paul as exemplary in their love for the Scriptures the most likely explanation for the fact that Timothy was not circumcised is that his father had forbidden it. In those days, wives normally had no choice but to do what their husbands ordered." [39]

Paul circumcised Timothy because of the Jews. Wade wrote: "Paul wanted to take him along as they continued their journey. But a problem arose: Timothy was uncircumcised. According to Jewish thinking, Timothy would have been considered a Jew because his mother was Jewish. Yet because he had not been circumcised, he would not have been acceptable to the Jews." [40]

David Lipscomb further explains, "Timothy, as the son of a Jewess, could be circumcised to identify him with the Jewish family. No one demanded that Timothy should be circumcised as a religious duty." [41] The rite of circumcision did not originate with the Law of Moses but with Abraham's family. (Genesis 17:9-14) The apostle Paul concluded in Galatians 5:6, "For in Christ Jesus neither circumcision nor uncircumcision avails anything; but faith which works by love."

It was probably at this time that the elders appointed Timothy to mission work (1 Timothy 4:14), and that Paul imparted to him the gift of prophecy (2 Timothy 1:6). Timothy became a great blessing to Paul and the church.

---

[39] David L. Roper, *Truth for Today Commentary, Acts 15-28,* p. 46-47
[40] John W. Wade, *Acts,* p. 165
[41] David Lipscomb, *A Commentary on the Acts of the Apostles,* p. 146

The Second Missionary Journey | 121

And as they went through the cities, they delivered to them the decrees to keep, that were ordained of the apostles and elders which were at Jerusalem. 16:4

This was the letter from the church in Jerusalem that rejected the requirement being taught by some that the Gentiles must be circumcised. (See Acts 15:23-29.) And Silas, who was from Jerusalem, was confirming the message that was in the letter.

And so were the churches established in the faith, and increased in number daily. 16:5

Paul's letter to these Galatians condemned those who would bind the Law of Moses upon the Gentiles. Silas and the letter from Jerusalem supported Paul's teachings, and so the churches were strengthened in the faith and grew also in number. In addition to Derbe and Lystra, they strengthened the churches in Iconium and Antioch of Pisidia.

Now when they had gone throughout Phrygia and the region of Galatia, they were forbidden of the Holy Spirit to preach the word in Asia. 16:6

The Holy Spirit did not allow them to evangelize the Roman province of Asia at this time. However, Paul would spend three years in Ephesus, the capital of Asia, on his third missionary journey. (Acts 20:17-18, 31)

After they were come to Mysia, they attempted to go into Bithynia, but the Spirit did not allow them. And passing by Mysia, they came down to Troas. 16:7

The Holy Spirit was leading them to Troas, a chief city of Mysia on the coast of the Aegean Sea opposite Greece.

And a vision appeared to Paul in the night. A man of Macedonia stood and pleaded with him, saying, "Come

over to Macedonia and help us." Now after he had seen the vision, immediately we sought to go to Macedonia, concluding that the Lord had called us to preach the gospel to them." NKJV 16:9-10**

Directly north of Greece was Macedonia, from where the Greek culture had been spread by Alexander the Great throughout the world. In a vision, Paul saw a man of Macedonia begging for help! Jesus Christ was directing the advancement of his kingdom into Europe.

Luke is now writing "we" and "us" instead of "they" and "them." He has joined Paul's missionary team at Troas. Paul now has three co-workers: Silas the older prophet, Timothy the young prophet, and Luke the physician (Colossians 4:14).

Therefore, loosing from Troas, we came with a straight course to Samothrace, and the next day to Neapolis. And from there to Philippi, which is the chief city of that part of Macedonia and a colony; and we were in that city abiding certain days. 16:11-12

Philippi was the city where the Lord wanted the gospel to be preached. Paul later would describe the church that was established at Philippi as his "joy and crown." (Philippians 4:1) He was thankful for their "fellowship in the gospel." (Philippians 1:3-5) They had given him financial support while he was there and when he went to other places. The city of Philippi, as a Roman colony, did not have to pay taxes to Rome. The citizens spoke Latin instead of Greek, wore Roman clothing and observed Roman customs. Roper concludes, "In Philippi, Paul was immersed in Roman culture in a way he had never been before. Perhaps his desire to go to Rome originated in Philippi. The Macedonian call was more than a call to a single Roman province; but it was a cry for help from a world lost in sin. Philippi represented the even greater challenge of reaching the entire Roman Empire." [42]

And on the Sabbath day we went outside the gate to a riverside, where we were supposing that there would be a place of prayer; and we sat down and began speaking to the women who had assembled. NASB **16:13**

There was no synagogue in Philippi because there were not enough Jewish men; ten were required to form a synagogue. [43]

And a certain woman named Lydia, a seller of purple, of the city of Thyatira, who worshiped God, heard us; whose heart the Lord opened, that she attended to the things which were spoken by Paul. 16:14

Lydia was a seller of purple dyed fabric that only the wealthy could afford. She was from Thyatira, a city known for its purple cloth. The church at Thyatira was one of the seven churches of Asia to whom the book of Revelation was addressed. (Revelation 1:4, 11) Lydia is described as one "who worshiped God," which usually referred to a Gentile God-fearer or proselyte. Lydia was paying close attention to the things Paul was saying. Roper notes, "Lydia was able to listen attentively to Paul *before* her heart was opened; no Calvinist doctrine is taught in the passage." [44] The Lord opened Lydia's heart through the agency of the gospel that was being preached, just like he did on Pentecost. (Acts 2:37) The word of God is a living and powerful two-edged sword that opens hearts (Hebrews 4:14); it is called "the sword of the Spirit" in Ephesians 6:17. Paul was not allowed to preach in Asia, but his first convert in Philippi was Lydia, who was from the Roman province of Asia.

---

[42] David L. Roper, *Truth for Today Commentary, Acts 15-28*, p. 57-58
[43] Ibid., p, 59
[44] Ibid., p. 61

And when she was baptized, and her household, she besought us, saying, "If you have judged me to be faithful to the Lord, come into my house and abide there. And she constrained us." 16:15

Lydia, being a seller of purple cloth, was probably wealthy and had a large house for all who worked with and for her. She showed her hospitality by inviting the four missionaries into her home; and she showed her propriety by saying, "If you have judged me to be faithful to the Lord."

Now it happened, as we went to prayer, that a certain slave girl met us, who brought her masters much profit by fortune-telling. This girl followed Paul and us, and cried out, saying, "These men are the servants of the Most High God, who proclaim to us the way of salvation." NJKV **16:16-17**

Paul and his co-workers were going to the "place of prayer" by the riverside to worship and to teach others as they had previously done. The girl was possessed with a demonic spirit like those that recognized Jesus as the Son of God. (Luke 8:26-28) So, the unclean spirit in the girl told the truth about the missionaries and their mission.

This she did many days. But Paul, being grieved, turned and said to the spirit, "I command you in the name of Jesus Christ to come out of her." And he came out the same hour. 16:18

Paul followed the example set by Jesus in casting out demonic spirits, even though they spoke the truth. The saving gospel of Christ was not to be associated with demons. The missionaries were not in an alliance with unclean spirits. Jesus had compassion upon the man possessed with many demons in Luke 8:33-39. Paul showed mercy for the girl by casting out the demon.

And when her masters saw that the hope of their gains was gone, they caught Paul and Silas and dragged them into the marketplace to the rulers. And they brought them to the magistrates, saying, "These men, being Jews, do exceedingly trouble our city and teach customs, which are not lawful for us to receive, neither to observe, being Romans." 16:19-21

The masters of the slave girl seized only Paul and Silas. Timothy and Luke may not have been present at this time, or they may have considered only Paul and Silas to be the leaders. They brought them before the rulers, who were in charge of the Roman colony. Their complaint was not their real motive. They accused Paul and Silas of being Jewish troublemakers, who were teaching customs that Romans could not receive or observe. Most Romans did not like the Jews. So, they were making it a racial issue to stir up prejudice rather than revealing their real motive—money. Some people become enemies of the truth when it causes them to lose money.

And the multitude rose up together against them; and the magistrates tore off their clothes and commanded to beat them. And when they had laid many stripes upon them, they cast them into prison, charging the jailer to keep them safely. Having received such a charge, he thrust them into the inner prison, and made their feet fast in stocks. 16:22-24

This was the first persecution of Christians provoked by Gentiles. The jailer made them as secure as possible; he put them in the inner prison with their feet in stocks.

And at midnight Paul and Silas prayed and sang praises to God, and the prisoners heard them. 16:25

Instead of complaining about unjust treatment, their faith caused them to pray that their suffering might lead others to believe. Persecution gave them the opportunity for witnessing to others about Christ. (Luke 21:12-13) And the other prisoners heard them praise God in songs.

And suddenly there was a great earthquake, so that the foundations of the prison were shaken; and immediately all the doors were opened, and everyone's chains were loosed. 16:26

The Lord was demonstrating his great power and authority. Roman rulers can beat his preachers publicly and place them in the most secure part of the prison, but Jesus Christ has the power to free them and to keep the other prisoners from escaping.

And the keeper of the prison, awaking out of his sleep and seeing the prison doors open, drew his sword and would have killed himself, supposing that the prisoners had fled. But Paul cried out with a loud voice, saying, "Do yourself no harm, for we are all here," 16:27-28

When Peter escaped from prison, the guards were questioned and killed by Herod. (Acts 12:3-19) The jailer at Philippi was about to take his own life rather than being humiliated, scourged, and killed by the authorities. But Paul prevented the jailer's suicide by letting him know that none of the prisoners had escaped.

Then he called for a light, and sprang in, and came trembling, and fell down before Paul and Silas. And he brought them out, and said, "Sirs, what must I do to be saved?" 16:30

Surely, he had heard about the slave girl, who said, "These men are servants of the Most High God, who show to us the way of salvation." He had not believed it, thinking Paul and Silas were just Jewish troublemakers. But now, seeing the great power that was with them, he believed that they were servants of God, and he wanted to know how to be saved. Wade wrote, "He may not have been absolutely sure of what Paul and Silas had to offer, but whatever it was, he knew he wanted it." [45]

And they said, "Believe on the Lord Jesus Christ, and you shall be saved, and your house." And they spoke to him the word of the Lord and to all that were in his house. 16:31-32

To be saved, one must believe on Jesus Christ as Lord. Being a Gentile, the jailer knew little or nothing about Jesus, so they spoke the word of the Lord to him and to all in his household, so they could believe. "Faith comes by hearing, and hearing by the word of God." (Romans 10:17) Just as the Samaritans needed to have Christ preached to them (Acts 8:5-12) and the Ethiopian official had to hear about Jesus (Acts 8:35-39), so the jailer and his household also needed to hear about Jesus Christ before they could believe.

And he took them the same hour of the night, and washed their stripes, and was baptized, he and all his family immediately. And when he had brought them into his house, he set food before them and rejoiced, believing with all his house. 16:33-34

His washing the wounds of Paul and Silas showed repentance. He and his family were baptized immediately during the night, showing the importance of baptism. Rejoicing came after baptism. All the members of his family were old enough to believe. The jailer was described as **believing in God with all his house**. This is not an example of infant baptism as some teach. Whenever Jesus Christ was preached, those who believed were baptized; and then they rejoiced. Infants are not capable of believing and rejoicing after baptism.

And when it was daylight, the magistrates sent their officers to the jailer with the order; "Release those men."

---

[45] John W. Wade, *Acts*, p. 174

The jailer told Paul, "The magistrates have ordered that you and Silas be released. Now you can leave. Go in peace," NIV **16:35-36**

The earthquake during the night may have caused the magistrates to believe that Paul and Silas could be "servants of the Most High God" as the slave girl had said. But they wanted them to leave Philippi as soon as possible. The riotous mob, that had demanded their punishment, might think that Paul and Silas had escaped because of the earthquake. These magistrates were more concerned about keeping the peace, than they were with truth and justice.

But Paul said to the officers, "They beat us publicly without a trial, even though we are Roman citizens, and threw us into prison. And now do they want to get rid of us quietly? No! Let them come themselves and escort us out." NIV **16:36-37**

Paul charged the magistrates with three violations of Roman justice: (1) beating Roman citizens, (2) failing to give them a trial, and (3) putting them in prison. Paul and Silas had not committed a crime; the magistrates had yielded to mob pressure. To beat a Roman citizen was unlawful; and Paul was born with Roman citizenship. (Acts 22:25-28) Silas probably obtained his citizenship in the same way, because his full name was Silvanus, a Latin name. Paul and Peter refer to him as Silvanus in their letters. [46] Silas is a short form of Silvanus.

The sergeants told these words to the magistrates; and they feared, when they heard that they were Romans. And they came and besought them and brought them out." 16:38

The magistrates could lose their jobs or even their lives for their unlawful acts. So, these chief officials came to the

---

[46] 2 Cor. 2:19; 1 Thess. 1:1; 2 Thess. 1:1; and 1 Peter 5:12

prison to release Paul and Silas. They were apologizing and begging them not to press charges against them. Paul and Silas had been punished publicly as criminals; and for the future success of the gospel of Christ in Philippi and elsewhere, Paul had demanded that their acquittal and release be just as public. Paul did not want the public to think of them as escaped criminals. He was not seeking personal revenge; so, he would not bring charges against the magistrates.

And they went out of the prison and entered into the house of Lydia. And when they had seen the brethren, they comforted them and departed. 16:40

Lydia's large house appears to be the meeting place of the church. Paul and Silas may have reminded the brethren of these words of Jesus: "In the world you shall have tribulation. But be of good cheer! I have overcome the world." (John 16:33) Did you notice that Luke writes, **"they ... departed**." Luke was not with Paul and Silas when they left Philippi and journeyed westward. Luke remained in Philippi to strengthen the church. The "we" statements do not appear again until Paul came through Philippi at the end of his third journey; and Luke wrote, "And we sailed away from Philippi." (Acts 20:6)

NOTES

Thessalonica to Athens
Acts 17

They came to Thessalonica, where there was a synagogue of the Jews. 17:1

Thessalonica was the capital of the Roman province of Macedonia; it was located about 100 miles southwest of Philippi. Being a center of commerce, it had a large Jewish population with a synagogue. The city is called Salonika today, and it is the major seaport for northern Greece.

And according to Paul's custom, he went to them, and for three Sabbaths reasoned with them from the Scriptures, explaining and giving evidence that the Christ had to suffer and rise again from the dead, and saying, "This Jesus whom I am proclaiming to you is the Christ." And some of them were persuaded and joined Paul and Silas, along with a great multitude of the God-fearing Greeks and a number of the leading women. NASB **17:2-4**

Paul's custom was to go first to the synagogues, because Jews and God-fearing Gentiles were expecting the Messiah. Paul was able to teach in their synagogue and show evidence from the Old Testament Scriptures that the Christ had to suffer and be raised from the dead. Jesus had fulfilled the messianic prophecies. A great number of the God-fearing Gentiles were receptive to the gospel of Christ; and even some of the Jews believed.

But the Jews, becoming jealous and taking along some wicked men from the marketplace, formed a mob and set the city in an uproar; and coming upon the house of Jason, they were seeking to bring them to the people. NASB **17:5**

The majority of the Jews rejected Paul's teachings, and they were jealous of him because so many of the Greeks believed. So, they created an uproar in the city and came to the house of Jason thinking that Paul and Silas were there.

And when they did not find them, they drew Jason and certain brethren to the rulers of the city, crying, "These that have turned the world upside down are come here also, whom Jason has received; and these all do contrary to the decrees of Caesar, saying that there is another king, one Jesus." And they troubled the people and the rulers of the city when they heard these things. And when they had taken security of Jason and of the others, they let them go. 17:6-9

They were bringing the same false charge against Paul and Silas that their rulers in Jerusalem had brought against Jesus before Pilate. Jesus was not a rival of Caesar. His kingdom is not of this world. (John 18:36)

This uproar did not take place immediately after Paul's three weeks of teaching in the synagogue. Paul and Silas did manual labor while there (1 Thess. 2:9); and the church at Philippi sent gifts to Paul for his necessities at Thessalonica at least twice. (Philippians 4:16)

The city rulers took securities from Jason and the other brethren. It seems that the authorities were requiring that Paul and Silas be sent away, and the securities would be returned to the brethren whenever the two men left their city. This conclusion is based on the next verse.

Then the brethren immediately sent Paul and Silas away by night to Berea. When they arrived, they went into the synagogue of the Jews. These were more fair-minded than those in Thessalonica, in that they received

the word with all readiness, and searched the Scriptures daily to find out whether these things were so." NKJV 17:10-11

Berea was about 50 miles southwest of Thessalonica. The Jews in Berea were more receptive to the gospel of Christ than the Jews in Thessalonica. However, many Gentiles along with some Jews in Thessalonica did receive God's word and believed. Paul wrote words of praise to the faithful Christians at Thessalonica, saying, "When you received the word of God which you heard from us, you received it not as the word of men, but as it is in truth, the word of God, the word which effectually works also in you that believe." (1 Thessalonians 2:13) The Bereans left us a great example to follow. We should always search the Scriptures to see if the things we have heard are true.

Many of them believed, also of honorable women who were Greeks, and of men not a few. 17:12

Both men and women will believe, when they receive God's word with an open mind and search the Scriptures. Even those of high rank of various cultures will believe.

But when the Jews of Thessalonica had knowledge that the word of God was preached by Paul at Berea, they came there also and stirred up the people. And then immediately the brethren sent Paul to go as it were to sea, but Silas and Timothy remained there. 17:13-14

These Jews had the same zeal to persecute Paul from city to city as those in Galatia. Paul may have recalled how he had persecuted Christians from city to city. We don't know how long it took for the Jews in Thessalonica to learn of Paul's work in Berea, but he was there long enough to establish a strong church. The brethren wisely had Paul to escape by the sea, which would call off the search for him by his enemies. Silas and Timothy stayed at Berea to strengthen the church in the faith. To secure Paul's safe passage, some of the brethren went with him to Athens. Before they returned to Berea, Paul sent a message with them for Silas and Timothy to come to him as soon as possible. **17:15**

Now while Paul waited for them in Athens, his spirit was stirred in him, when he saw the city wholly given to idolatry. 17:16

Paul was alone in the learning center of the ancient world. Athens was the seat of Greek culture, with its great art, architecture, philosophy and science. However, Paul was not impressed with its beauty and learning, but he was depressed with its idolatry.

Therefore, he disputed in the synagogue with the Jews and with the devout persons, and in the market daily with those that met with him. 17:17

Paul taught the Jews and God-fearing Gentiles in the synagogue, and was daily in the marketplace talking with people.

When Silas and Timothy arrived in Athens, their time with Paul was brief. Paul was concerned for the churches in Thessalonica and Berea. He wanted to know how the brethren in Thessalonica were doing. So, he sent Timothy to them. A few months later, Paul wrote to them, saying, "When we could no longer forbear, we thought it good to be left at Athens alone, and sent Timothy, our brother, and minister of God, and our fellow-laborer in the gospel to establish you and comfort you in the faith; that no man should be moved by these afflictions." (1 Thess. 3:1-3) Silas went back to Berea, because when Paul left Athens, he departed alone. Paul did not see his two co-workers again until they came from Macedonia to him at Corinth.

Then certain philosophers of the Epicureans and of the Stoics encountered him. 17:18

The Epicureans said that man's goal in life was to seek pleasure through his natural inclinations and passions; this view degenerated into "Let's eat, drink, and be merry, for tomorrow we die." The Stoics believed that fate determined everything and that the greatest good in life was in being indifferent to both sorrows and joys; they emphasized the importance of self-discipline and doing one's duty in life. Both philosophies denied a conscious life after death.

Some said, "What does this babbler want to say?" Others said, "He seems to be a proclaimer of foreign gods," because he preached to them Jesus and the resurrection. NKJV **17:18**

The Greek word translated **babbler** literally means "seed-picker," referring to birds that survived by picking up seeds here and there. "Later, it was applied to persons who developed their philosophy by taking a bit from one school and a bit from another and combining them and pretending it was something new." [47]

And they took him, and brought him to Areopagus, saying, "May we know what this new doctrine is of which you speak? For you bring certain strange things to our ears; we would know what these things mean." (For all the Athenians and strangers who were there spent their time in nothing else, but either to tell or to hear some new thing.) 17:19-21

Areopagus means Ares Hill. Ares was the Greek god of war. (It is also called Mars Hill; Mars was the Latin god of war.) Ares Hill was a small rocky hill west of the Acropolis, the high flat hill on which stood the Parthenon, the temple to the goddess Athena. Both Ares Hill and the Acropolis were

---

[47] John W. Wade, *Acts*, p. 182

south of the marketplace, called the agora. In earlier days, the highest court of Athens always met on Ares Hill, the Areopagus, which gave this court its name. Even in Paul's time, on special occasions, the court met on the hill, but their regular meetings were held in a colonnade in the agora. Since "Areopagus" can refer both to the court and to the hill, Paul could have been taken to either place. Paul was not on trial before the Areopagus; they only were interested in hearing something new.

Then Paul stood in the midst of the Areopagus and said, "Men of Athens, I perceive that in all things you are very religious; for as I was passing through and considering the objects of your worship, I even found an altar with this inscription: TO THE UNKNOWN GOD. Therefore, the One whom you worship without knowing, Him I proclaim to you." NKJV **17:22-23**

Paul used their own altar to "the unknown god" to begin his sermon about the true God, whom they worshiped in ignorance. Paul was not a "seed picker" borrowing from others; he would reveal the Creator of all things to them.

"God who made the world and all things therein, seeing that he is Lord of heaven and earth, dwells not in temples made with hands; neither is worshiped with men's hands as though he needed anything seeing that he gives to all life and breath and all things." 17:24-25

Roper writes, "Paul was telling them that they had not made God, but God had made them; they had not made God a home, but He had made them a home—this earth. Paul was surrounded by the greatest array of pagan temples the world has ever seen. God, however, had no need of temples, regardless of how beautiful they were. Unlike the lifeless, helpless idols in those temples, God did not need the

Athenians to serve Him; rather, they needed God's help." [48] We cannot live without God, our Creator.

"He has made of one every nation of mankind to live on all the face of the earth, having determined their appointed times and the boundaries of their habitation, that they should seek God, if perhaps they might grope for Him and find Him, though He is not far from each one of us." [NASB] **17:26-27**

All races came from one family, and Eve is the mother of all living. (Gen. 3:20) All nations of the earth came from the family of Noah. (Gen. 10:32) Roper makes the following observations: "The Greeks thought of themselves as unique, with a different origin and status than all other men. They grouped mankind into 'Greeks and barbarians.' Most ethnic groups thought of mankind as composed of 'us' and 'them.' Such prejudicial groupings continue among those unaware that Jesus broke down the barriers between men (Eph. 2:14), so we might all be 'one in Christ Jesus' (Gal. 3:26-28). The only categories that really matter are 'in Christ' and 'outside of Christ.'" [49]

Nations rise and fall at God's appointed times, for he determines the boundaries of nations. (Daniel 8:19; 11:27; Hab. 2:3) "The Most High rules in the kingdoms of men." (Daniel 4:17) "He changes the times and the seasons; he removes kings and sets up kings." (Daniel 2:21) Nebuchadnezzar king of Babylon learned this truth, and he wrote, "Now I Nebuchadnezzar praise and extol and honor the King of heaven, all whose works are truth and his ways judgment; and those that walk in pride he is able to abase." (Daniel 4:37)

---

[48] David Roper, *Truth for Today Commentary, Acts 15-28,* p. 113
[49] Ibid., p, 113

If men do not acknowledge the one true God in their search for truth, they are groping in the dark as blind men. Paul was telling these philosophers in Athens that they could know the living God. If they would seek the Lord, the one they called the UNKNOWN GOD, they could find him for he is near. Later, Paul wrote in Romans 1:20, "For since the creation of the world His invisible attributes, His eternal power and divine nature, have been clearly seen, being understood through what he has made, so that they are without excuse. For even though they knew God, they did not honor Him as God, or give thanks; but they became futile in their speculations, and their foolish heart was darkened. Professing to be wise, they became fools." NASB

"For in him we live, and move, and have our being; as certain also of your own poets have said, 'For we are also his offspring.'" 17:28

In Colossians 1:16-17, Paul writes, "All things were created by Him and for Him; and He is before all things, and by Him all things consist." Hebrews 1:3 says that He is "upholding all things by the word of his power."

David Roper writes, "Paul quoted from two poets. His previous thought had been expressed years earlier in a poem attributed to Epimenides (c. 600 B.C.): 'In thee we live and move and have our being.' The second quotation, 'we also are His children,' apparently referred to a line from the writings of Aratus (born 310 B.C.): 'For we are truly his offspring.' Aratus was a Cilician as Paul was. Paul probably had often heard the words of Aratus quoted during his early schooling in Tarsus. It should be noted that the god referred to in these poems was not Jehovah, who was 'unknown' to them, but their principal god, Zeus. Paul was not saying that Jehovah is to be identified with Zeus. Rather, he was pointing out that even human philosophy had led to the concept of a close, personal God, and therefore, that his words about the nature of the true God should not be thought unreasonable." [50]

Forasmuch then as we are the offspring of God, we ought not to think that the Godhead is like unto gold, or silver, or stone, graven by art and man's device." 17:29

Children are like their parents. God created man in his own image (Genesis 1:17) and provides for man. (v. 25) Being the offspring of God, why should we worship a lifeless sculpture created by man? Regardless of how beautiful the work of art, it cannot think, see, hear, speak, or feel, and men must provide for it. (cf. Isaiah 44:9-17) The word "Godhead" in the KJV refers to deity, and the Greek is translated Divine Nature in other translations.

The times of ignorance God overlooked, but now he commands all people everywhere to repent, because he has fixed a day on which he will judge the world in righteousness by a man whom he has appointed, and of this he has given assurance to all by raising him from the dead." [ESV] **17:30-31**

The true God has made the world and all things. The worship of lifeless idols is unreasonable. Paul exposed the ignorance of the world's greatest thinkers. And now God calls upon them to repent of their ignorance and their idolatry. All people everywhere must repent of sins, because God has appointed a judgment day for the whole world, and he has appointed a judge who will judge in righteousness. "We must all appear before the judgment seat of Christ." (2 Cor. 5:10) We are assured of the Judgment Day, because God has raised Jesus Christ from the dead.

---

[50] Roper, Ibid., pp. 115-116

And when they heard of the resurrection of the dead, some mocked, and others said, "We will hear you again of this matter." 17:32

Paul was ready to tell them about Jesus, but they would not listen. His speaking of the resurrection was too foolish for these intellectuals who worshiped lifeless idols. When Paul wrote about the foolishness of human wisdom, he was reflecting upon his experience in Athens. (1 Cor. 1:18 – 2:5)

So, Paul departed from among them. However, some men joined him and believed, among them Dionysius the Areopagite, a woman name Damaris, and others. NKJV **17:33-34**

This shows Paul was not on trial; he was free to go as he chose. Jesus had taught his disciples, "Whoever shall not receive you, nor hear you, when you depart out of that house or city, shake off the dust of your feet" (Matthew 10:14), and "Give not that which is holy to the dogs, neither cast your pearls before swine." (Matthew 7:6) Paul knew when it was time to leave.

Paul's teaching resulted in some believing, including a distinguished member of the Areopagus court, Dionysius. According to tradition, he became an elder in the church at Athens. [51] Damaris must have been an influential woman. Paul was not a failure at Athens as some have stated; he faithfully preached the word of God and souls were saved. His sermon is treasured by all those who know the true God, the Lord of heaven and earth.

---

[51] Roper, Ibid., p. 121

Corinth to Antioch
Acts 18

Paul departed from Athens, and came to Corinth. 18:1

Corinth was forty miles west of Athens. The city was located on the southwest end of the isthmus that connected the southern part of Greece with the northern part. Nine miles from Corinth was Cenchrea, the seaport to the east. Because of its location in Greece, the commerce of the world passed through Corinth from all four directions. Paul came to Corinth alone. Luke was in Philippi, Timothy in Thessalonica, and Silas perhaps in Berea.

Paul wrote to the Corinthians, "When I came to you ... I was with you in weakness, and in fear, and in much trembling." (1 Cor. 2:1, 3) He may have been physically exhausted, and he may have been suffering from his "thorn in the flesh." His funds likely were depleted, and he was seeking a job to support himself. He had been mocked and scorned at Athens. He had to flee from Berea and Thessalonica. He had suffered a beating and was placed in stocks in the prison at Philippi. What was awaiting him in Corinth?

Corinth was known for its commerce, but it was also known for its immorality. On a high mountain towering over the city was the temple of Aphrodite with her many prostitutes. This goddess of love was called Venus by the Romans. Even in other places, a "Corinthian girl" described a harlot, and a person of low morals was called "a Corinthian." Paul later wrote to the Corinthians, "Do not be deceived. Neither fornicators, nor idolaters, nor adulterers, nor homosexuals, nor sodomites, nor thieves, nor covetous, nor drunkards, nor revilers, nor extortioners will inherit the kingdom of God. And such were some of you. But you were washed, but you were sanctified, but you were justified in the name of the Lord Jesus and by the Spirit of our God." (1 Cor. 6:9-11) This was a wicked city in great need of the gospel. A large and varied population was in Corinth. Being alone, Paul must have felt overwhelmed by the task before him. But he was not alone, God was with him. And through the Holy Spirit's providence, Paul would find help.

And he found a certain Jew named Aquila, born in Pontus, lately come from Italy with his wife Priscilla (because Claudius had commanded all Jews to depart from Rome); and he came to them. 18:2

Paul found Aquila and Priscilla, who provided friendship and encouragement. This would be an enduring relationship. In Romans 16:3-4, Paul calls them "my helpers in Christ Jesus, who have for my life laid down their own necks." The couple had come to Corinth after being persecuted in Rome. The emperor Claudius had expelled all the Jews from Rome. John Wade says, "The Roman historian Suetonius reports rioting in Rome at the 'instigation of one Chrestos.' Some scholars understand this to refer to followers of Christ, whose appearance in Rome caused violence among the Jews, just as it had in the provinces. Some even go so far as to claim that Aquila and Priscilla were already Christians when Paul first met them. Of course, we have no definite proof of this. It is interesting to note that although they later became faithful co-workers with Paul, no mention is made of their conversion, lending some support to the speculation. This Jewish couple provided Paul with a place to stay and companionship until Silas and Timothy arrived." [52]

---

[52] John W. Wade, *Acts*, pp. 190-191

Aquila is a Roman name; so to keep us from thinking that he was a Gentile, Luke points out that he was a "Jew." Aquila was from Pontus originally; and Jews from Pontus heard Peter's sermon on the day of Pentecost. (Acts 2:9) This leads us to believe that Aquila and Priscilla were already Christians when they met Paul.

And because he was of the same craft, he stayed with them and worked; for by their occupation, they were tentmakers. 18:3

God provided the opportunity for Paul to work with his hands, which helps to relieve doubts and fears. Like most Jewish boys, Paul had been taught a trade, even though he was trained as a rabbi. His craft was tentmaking, the same as Aquila and Priscilla. Paul was able to support himself whenever he thought it best for the reception of the gospel. (1 Cor. 9:7-18) Because Aquila and Priscilla made tents, does not mean that they lived in a tent. When they went with Paul to Ephesus to help spread the gospel, they had a house in which the church met (1 Cor. 16:19); and when they went back to Rome, the church was meeting in their house (Romans 16:3-5).

And he reasoned in the synagogue every Sabbath and persuaded the Jews and the Greeks. 18:4

God also provided a place for Paul to preach. The Greeks were those who attended the synagogue services to learn more about God. As he did in Thessalonica, Paul was trying to convince both the Jews and the Greeks that the Scriptures taught the Christ must suffer and rise again from the dead. (Acts 17:2-3; Isaiah 53)

But when Silas and Timothy came down from Macedonia, Paul began devoting himself completely to the word, solemnly testifying to the Jews that Jesus is the Christ." NASB **18:5**

Paul was able to devote fulltime to preaching the word, because of the financial support he received with the arrival of Silas and Timothy, along with "the brethren who came from Macedonia." (2 Cor. 11:9) These brethren were from Philippi, because Paul wrote to the Philippians, "When I departed from Macedonia, no church shared with me concerning the giving and receiving but you only." (Philippians 4:15) After showing that the Christ must suffer, die, and be raised, Paul now boldly testified that Jesus is the Christ. In 1 Corinthians 15:1-4, Paul makes known the gospel that he preached to the Corinthians.

And when they resisted and blasphemed, he shook out his garments and said to them, "Your blood be upon your own heads! I am clean. From now on I shall go to the Gentiles." And he departed from there and went to the house of a certain man named Titius Justus, a worshiper of God, whose house was next to the synagogue. NASB **18:6-7**

The Jews resisted Paul and blasphemed Jesus. Paul's saying, "Your blood be upon your own heads! I am clean," is a reference to Ezekiel 33:4-8. Shaking the dust off his clothing sent the message that God was rejecting them, because they had rejected him.

When cast out by the Jews, Paul went next door to the house of Titius Justus, who worshiped God. After listening to Paul in the synagogue, this Gentile welcomed the gospel message. Titus is the short form of Titius. But this is not the Titus of Antioch, who was already a Christian at the time of the Jerusalem meeting (Acts 15), according to Galatians 2:3.

And Crispus, the chief ruler of the synagogue, believed on the Lord with all his house. And many of the Corinthians, hearing, believed and were baptized. 18:8

When Paul left the synagogue, its chief ruler and his family went with him. Their acceptance of the gospel must have been very encouraging to Paul. But it was also alarming to the unbelieving Jews. Crispus was among the few that were personally baptized by Paul. (1 Cor. 1:14) As Paul continued to preach in the house of Justus, "many of the Corinthians, hearing, believed, and were baptized." This is how people are saved when the gospel of Christ is preached. (Mark 16:15-16)

Then spoke the Lord to Paul in the night by a vision, "Be not afraid, but speak, and hold not your peace: for I am with you, and no man shall set on you to hurt you, for I have much people in this city." And he continued there a year and six months, teaching the word of God. 18:9-11

Paul must have been fearing the riotous reaction of unbelieving Jews as in other cities. But in a night vision, the Lord assured him that he would be with him and protect him from harm. Paul needed to speak boldly without fear, because many people would believe if given the opportunity to hear the gospel. With this assurance, Paul stayed in Corinth for a year and a half. During this time, Paul wrote First and Second Thessalonians.

But while Gallio was proconsul of Achaia, the Jews with one accord rose up against Paul and brought him before the judgment seat, saying, "This man persuades men to worship God contrary to the law." But when Paul was about to open his mouth, Gallio said to the Jews, "If this were a matter of wrong or of vicious crime, O Jews, it would be reasonable for me to put up with you; but if there are questions about words and names and your own law, look after it yourselves; I am unwilling to be a judge of these matters." And he drove them away from the judgment seat. And they all took hold of Sosthenes, the

leader of the synagogue, and began beating him in front of the judgment seat. But Gallio was not concerned about any of these things." ^{NASB} 18:12-17

Roper writes, "The Jews did not bring Paul before city magistrates as had been the case in other cities, but before the governor of the entire province of **Achaia**, of which Corinth was the capital. An adverse ruling by a powerful man like Gallio would set a precedent for all other Roman provinces. The legal and political significance of this event cannot be over-emphasized."[53] Gallio thought of the Jews as troublemakers, since he speaks of putting up with them in verse 14. Reese writes, "Having come to Corinth from Rome, Gallio would have been acquainted with the 'Chrestus' over which the Jews at Rome were fighting; and in the charges against Paul, Gallio is hearing some of the same things he had heard a few years before at Rome."[54] So, he removed the Jews from his court. When the new leader of the synagogue, Sosthenes, was beaten up, Gallio probably thought that he received what he deserved for troubling his court. In 1 Corinthians 1:1, Paul says "Sosthenes our brother" was with him. If this is the same Sosthenes, then another synagogue ruler became a Christian.

Paul, having remained many days longer, took leave of the brethren and put out to sea for Syria, and with him were Priscilla and Aquila. At Cenchrea he had his hair cut, for he was keeping a vow. ^{NASB} **18:18**

During the days after his trial before Gallio, Paul was able to reach many people with the gospel just as the Lord had promised. Because of his extended stay in Corinth, there were saints throughout Achaia. (2 Cor. 1:1) Paul, writing to the Romans from Corinth, said, "Erastus, the treasurer of the city, greets you." ^{NKJV} (Romans 16:23) Paul

---

[53] David L. Roper, *Truth for Today Commentary, 15-28*, p. 148
[54] Gareth L. Reese, *New Testament History— Acts*, p. 649

also mentions Erastus in 2 Timothy 4:20. Paul decided it was time to return to Antioch in Syria. At Cenchrea, the eastern seaport of Corinth, Paul had his hair cut due to a vow he had made, possibly when the Lord appeared to him in the vision at night assuring him that he would be with him and that no one would hurt him.

Priscilla and Aquila were going with Paul part of the way. Silas and Timothy were staying with the church in Corinth. Silas is last mentioned in Acts when he came to Corinth. (18:5) Silas later worked with Peter, and with the help of Silas, Peter wrote his first letter. (1 Pet. 5:12)

And he came to Ephesus and left them there. But he himself entered into the synagogue and reasoned with the Jews. When they desired him to tarry a longer time with them, he consented not. But he bade them farewell, saying, "I must by all means keep this feast that comes in Jerusalem, but I will return again to you, if God wills. And he sailed from Ephesus. 18:19-21

Paul left Aquila and Priscilla at Ephesus, the capital of the Roman province of Asia, to prepare the people for his return visit. While waiting for his boat to sail, Paul entered the synagogue and lectured to the Jews. They desired him to stay longer, but he wanted to go to a feast in Jerusalem, not out of religious duty, but in order to see those that would be there. He promised to return to Ephesus, if the Lord was willing.

And when he had landed at Caesarea and gone up and greeted the church, he went down to Antioch. 18:22

Caesarea was Judea's major seaport. Paul traveled south and went up in elevation to the city of Jerusalem, where he visited with the church. And then he went north and down in elevation to the city of Antioch in Syria.

And after he had spent some time there, he departed and went over all the country of Galatia and Phrygia in order, strengthening the disciples. 18:23

Paul was beginning his third missionary journey.

A certain Jew named Apollos, born at Alexandria, an eloquent man and mighty in the Scriptures, came to Ephesus. 18:24

We are introduced to Apollos, who was from the large Jewish community in Alexandria, Egypt. The Septuagint, a Greek translation of the Old Testament, had been made there. Alexandria rivaled Athens as a center of learning. Apollos was well-educated and eloquent. Knowing the Old Testament Scriptures, he had power to reason and to persuade.

This man had been instructed in the way of the Lord; and being fervent in spirit, he was speaking and teaching accurately the things concerning Jesus, being acquainted only with the baptism of John. NASB **18:25**

Apollos' knowledge of Jesus was limited to the teachings of John the Baptist. Roper notes, "John had been killed (Mt. 14:1-12) before Jesus promised to build His church (Mt. 16:16-19)—and *long* before Jesus died, was raised, gave the Great Commission, and ascended to heaven." [55]

Apollos may have learned the teachings of John in more recent years from a disciple of John. John the Baptist came to prepare the way for the Christ, according to Isaiah 40:3 and Malachi 4:5-6. His was "a baptism of repentance" to prepare people for the coming of Christ. (Mark. 1:4) The baptism of the Great Commission is "in the name of the Father and of the Son and of the Holy Spirit" and is to be observed to the end of the Christian age. (Matthew 28:19-20) We are to be baptized into Christ's death. We are "buried with Him by baptism into death, that like as Christ was raised

---

[55] David L. Roper, Ibid., pp. 161-162

up from the dead by the glory of the Father, even so we also should walk in newness of life." (Romans 6:3-4) Now there is only "one baptism" (Ephesians 4:5). Roper notes, "A major short-coming of John's baptism was that it was predicated upon an incomplete knowledge of Jesus. John could only charge his followers 'to believe in Him who was coming after him' (Acts 19:4)." [56]

And he began to speak out boldly in the synagogue. But when Priscilla and Aquila heard him, they took him aside and explained to him the way of God more accurately. NASB **18:26**

They did not interrupt Apollos publicly, but they taught him privately. The Greek text mentions Priscilla first, indicating that she took the lead in the teaching. They demonstrated the ability to teach and to speak the truth in love. The learned may learn even more, even from those in their audience, if they are seeking the truth. This is a testimony to the humble character of Apollos.

And when he wanted to go across to Achaia, the brethren encouraged him and wrote to the disciples to welcome him; and when he arrived, he greatly helped those who had believed through grace, for he powerfully refuted the Jews in public, demonstrating by the Scriptures that Jesus was the Christ. NASB **18:27-28**

The letter by the brethren shows that there was at least a small congregation at Ephesus. It is likely that Priscilla and Aquila told Apollos about Corinth. He crossed over the Aegean Sea to arrive in Achaia. Apollos was a great blessing to the church at Corinth. Paul later would write, "I planted, Apollos watered, but God gave the increase." (1 Cor. 3:6)

---

[56] David L. Roper, Ibid., p. 163

NOTES

The Third Missionary Journey

Acts 19
Paul at Ephesus

While Apollos was at Corinth, Paul having passed through the higher regions came to Ephesus. 19:1

Paul began his third journey by leaving Antioch in Syria, and passing through Galatia, he visited the congregations he had established during his first journey. (18:22-23) As he traveled westward, Paul came down to Ephesus, which was on a river and only four miles from the Aegean Sea. All the commerce of that region flowed through the city. One of the seven wonders of the ancient world was there: the huge marble Temple of Artemis (Diana). Ephesus was the capital of the Roman province of Asia, and was also one of the great cities of the world.

And finding certain disciples, he said to them, "Have you received the Holy Spirit since you believed?" And they said to him, "We have not so much as heard whether there is any Holy Spirit." 19:1-2

Paul, being an apostle, had the power to impart "the gift of the Holy Spirit." (Acts 2:38) Since they were the only ones who could impart this gift, the apostles wanted to share these miraculous gifts with baptized believers to establish them in the faith. (Acts 8:14-17; Romans 1:11) However, these disciples at Ephesus had not heard of the Holy Spirit.

And he said, "Into what then were you baptized?" NASB **19:3** Paul realized that they had not been baptized with the baptism that Jesus had commanded, which is "in the name of the Father and of the Son and of the Holy Spirit." (Matthew 28:19)

And they said, "Into John's baptism." And Paul said, "John baptized with the baptism of repentance, telling the people to believe in Him who was coming after him, that is, in Jesus." NASB **19:3, 4**

These men may have been taught by Apollos or one of his followers. They believed that Jesus was the Christ, but they did not know the gospel of Christ: his death, burial and resurrection. They had not heard of Christ's ascension into heaven and the coming of the Holy Spirit on Pentecost to establish Christ's kingdom. John's baptism of repentance only prepared the people to believe in Jesus and obey him. Surely, Paul told them more about Jesus and his gospel than what Luke records in verse 4.

When they heard this, they were baptized in the name of the Lord Jesus. 19:5

They heard the gospel of Christ before they were baptized. This example shows the importance of baptism. It must be for the right purpose with faith in Jesus' death, burial and resurrection.

And when Paul laid his hands on them, the Holy Spirit came on them; and they spoke with tongues and they prophesied. And all the men were about twelve. 19:6-7

Again, we can see **when and how** the gift of the Holy Spirit was given. The gift was miraculous. They were speaking in languages previously unknown to them, and they were prophesying. This example shows that it was a common practice of the apostles to impart the miraculous gift of the Holy Spirit to baptized believers.

He went into the synagogue and spoke boldly for the space of three months, disputing and persuading the things concerning the kingdom of God. 19:8

The Third Missionary Journey | 153

Paul was able to speak in the synagogue at Ephesus longer than anywhere else: three months at Ephesus and only three weeks at Thessalonica. He may have been taking the time to review all of the Old Testament prophecies concerning the kingdom of God and the coming of the Messiah.

But when several were hardened and believed not, but spoke evil of that way before the multitude, he departed from them and separated the disciples, disputing daily in the school of one Tyrannus. And this continued by the space of two years; so that all they which dwelt in Asia heard the word of the Lord Jesus, both Jews and Greeks. 19:9-10

Our hearts are hardened when we repeatedly reject the truth. Many of the unbelieving Jews began to speak evil of Christianity before the synagogue crowd. So, Paul left the synagogue with his disciples and began teaching daily in the lecture hall of Tyrannus, who may have been a Christian. While in Ephesus, Paul also taught "from house to house" (20:20) and worked with his own hands to support himself (20:34). Tyrannus may have taught classes in the morning, while Paul was making tents in Aquila's workshop. In the afternoon hours, Paul could have taught in the school of Tyrannus. The evenings would be the time for teaching from house to house. Due to his teaching daily for two years, his disciples were able to spread the gospel throughout the whole province. Epaphras, who established the church at Colosse, was most likely one of his students. (Colossians 1:4-7)

And God was doing extraordinary miracles by the hands of Paul, so that even handkerchiefs or aprons that had touched his skin were carried to the sick, and their diseases left them and the evil spirits came out of them. ᴱˢⱽ **19:11-12**

Roper explains, "These were probably articles of clothing that had been in contact with Paul's body. The **handkerchiefs** were not small squares of cloth with hemmed edges, but large rags used by Paul, probably to wipe the sweat from his face as he made tents. He may have tied the rags around his head as was the custom. One translator called them 'sweat-rags,' another 'sweat-bands.' The **aprons** probably were the workman's apron worn by Paul to protect his clothing. These "extraordinary miracles" remind us of those who were healed when they touched Jesus' garments (Mark 5:25-29; 6:56)." [57]

Then certain of the vagabond Jews, exorcists, took upon themselves to call over them who had evil spirits the name of the Lord Jesus, saying, "We adjure you by Jesus, whom Paul preaches." And there were seven sons of one Sceva, a Jew and chief of the priests, who did so. And the evil spirit answered and said, "Jesus I know, and Paul I know; but who are you?" And the man, in whom the evil spirit was, leaped on them, and overcame them, and prevailed against them, so that they fled out of that house naked and wounded. And this was known to all the Jews and Greeks also dwelling in Ephesus; and fear fell on them all. And the name of the Lord was magnified. 19:13-17

These Jews claimed to be able to cast out evil spirits. Sceva was the chief of these false priests, his seven sons. When they saw or heard that Paul actually had the power to cast out evil spirits in the name of Jesus, they thought they might be successful if they tried this new incantation. But the evil spirit declared that he knew Jesus and Paul, but asked, "Who are you?" and brutally attacked them. This became known to all in Ephesus, and both Jews and Greeks were made aware of the power of the Lord Jesus.

---

[57] David L. Roper, *Truth for Today Commentary, Acts 15-28*, p. 186

And many who had believed came confessing and telling their deeds. Also, many of those who had practiced magic brought their books together and burned them in the sight of all. And they counted up the value of them and found it totaled fifty thousand pieces of silver. NKJV **19:18-19**

Those who believed in Jesus showed their faith by their works. (James 2:17-18) Ephesus was known for its trade in magical arts. [58] Many Christians had books of magic and astrology. Knowing the true power of God led them to confess their sins and publicly burn their books of magic, which were "filled with incantations, spells to bless or curse, recipes for love potions, formulas for casting out spirits, directions for foretelling the future, and so on." [59] Their books could have been sold for a great price. But these disciples were making a complete break with their past, and they did not want others to have these Satanic books. They set a good example for believers in Christ to follow, even for us today.

So mightily grew the word of God and prevailed. 19:20

The church at Ephesus grew in strength and in numbers, having elders to oversee the work. (20:17) While in Ephesus, Paul stayed in contact with the church at Corinth (1 Cor. 5:9) and even crossed the Aegean Sea for a brief visit. (2 Cor.12:14; 13:1) Roper notes, "These two references mention a *third* visit. This necessitates a second visit between the time Paul left Corinth at the end of the second journey (18:18) and his visit with them at the end of his third journey (20:2, 3). This certainly had to be while Paul was living and working in Ephesus." [60]

---

[58] Gareth L. Reese, *New Testament History—Acts*, p. 682
[59] Roper, Ibid., p. 190
[60] Roper, Ibid., p. 192

After these things Paul purposed in the spirit, when he had passed through Macedonia and Achaia to go to Jerusalem, saying, "After I have been there, I must also see Rome." 19:21

With the work going well at Ephesus, Paul began making plans for his future labors. Aquila and Priscilla were preparing to return to Rome, because we find them living in Rome when Paul wrote Romans from Corinth a year later. Paul planned to visit the churches he had established during his second missionary journey in Macedonia and Achaia. Then he would go to Jerusalem with their contributions for the poor saints. After that Paul wanted to go to Rome, where many of his fellow-workers had gone. (Romans 16:1-15)

So, he sent into Macedonia two of them that ministered to him, Timothy and Erastus; but he himself stayed in Asia for a season. 19:22

Timothy and Erastus must have come from Corinth to Ephesus to help Paul in his work, while Apollos was at Corinth. (19:1) Paul sent these men to Macedonia and Achaia to encourage the collections for the poor saints in Jerusalem. (1 Cor. 16:1) Earlier, Stephanas, Fortunatus, and Achaicus had come to Ephesus with a letter from the brethren at Corinth, containing questions for Paul to answer. (1 Cor. 16:17; 7:1) Paul had written 1 Corinthians in response and sent it to Corinth by these three men. Timothy was going by way of Macedonia to Corinth to see how they had received Paul's letter. (1 Cor. 4:17) In this letter to the Corinthians, Paul writes of his work at Ephesus: "I will tarry in Ephesus until Pentecost. For a great and effective door has opened to me, and there are many adversaries." NKJV (1 Corinthians 16:8-9) Soon the adversaries would become even greater.

About that time there arose no little disturbance concerning the Way. For a man named Demetrius, a silversmith, who made silver shrines of Artemis, brought

no little business to the craftsmen. These he gathered together, with the workmen in similar trades, and said, "Men, you know that from this business we have our wealth. And you see and hear that not only in Ephesus but in all of Asia this Paul has persuaded and turned away a great many people, saying that gods made with hands are not gods. And there is a danger not only that this trade of ours may come into disrepute but also that the temple of the great goddess Artemis may be counted as nothing, and that she may even be deposed from her magnificence, she whom all Asia and the world worship." When they heard this, they were enraged and were crying out, "Great is Artemis of the Ephesians!" ᴱˢⱽ 19:23-28

Luke again refers to Christianity as the Way. This disturbance against Christians came in the spring, because Paul was going to remain in Ephesus until Pentecost. The annual festival honoring Artemis was during the springtime. Artemis was the Greek mother-goddess, a fertility goddess. (Diana was the Roman goddess of fertility; the KJV incorrectly reflects the Latin Vulgate translation.) Her worshipers came to the festival from all over the province of Asia and beyond. Demetrius, a silversmith, made silver shrines of Artemis. Such shrines, made of marble or terra-cotta, have been unearthed. They are miniature models of the statue of Artemis inside her temple. Larger models were placed in the homes to be worshiped; smaller ones were worn as good-luck charms.[61] Demetrius and his craftsmen had a very profitable business.

But their sales had fallen off that year, due to fewer worshipers attending the festival. Demetrius gathered his craftsmen together, along with those who were making marble and terra-cotta shrines. His first concern was money. He spoke of Paul's success, not only in Ephesus but in all of

---

[61] Gareth L. Reese, *New Testament History—Acts*, pp.686-687

province of Asia, in turning a great many people away from the worship of Artemis and other gods crafted by man. If they did not get rid of Paul, they all would be out of work. His second concern was religion and patriotism. If the people quit worshiping Artemis, she would lose her glory; and her great temple, which was one of the Seven Wonders of the World, would become as nothing. Ephesus would lose its tourist trade.

Soon the whole city was in an uproar. The people seized Gaius and Aristarchus, Paul's traveling companions from Macedonia, and rushed as one man into the theater. Paul wanted to appear before the crowd, but the disciples would not let him. Even some of the officials of the province, friends of Paul, sent him a message begging him not to venture into the theater. NIV 19:29-32

As the craftsmen moved out into the street chanting, **"Great is Artemis of the Ephesians,"** others joined them in their march to the theater, an open-air stadium seating 25,000. The structure is still standing today. The marchers were a riotous mob in confusion. They found two of Paul's traveling companions, Gaius and Aristarchus, and brought them into the theater. Several men with the name Gaius are in the New Testament, and this Gaius from Macedonia may not be identified with any of the others with certainty. We know that Aristarchus was from Thessalonica (Acts 20:4); and later, he went with Paul to Jerusalem and was Paul's "fellow prisoner" in Rome. (Colossians 4:10; Philemon 24)

Fearing for the safety of Gaius and Aristarchus, Paul wanted to go into the assembly, but disciples would not let him. It was useless to try to reason with the mob, and the disciples could not afford to lose Paul. Even some of the officials of Asia who were Paul's friends warned him repeatedly not to go into the theater. Paul had friends in the government.

The Jews, denying any involvement with Paul, put forward Alexander to make their defense. But he was not allowed to speak, because he was a Jew. The Jews did not worship Artemis and other idols. So, for the next two hours the mob shouted: **"Great is Artemis of the Ephesians." 19:34**

When the town clerk had quieted the crowd, he said, "Men of Ephesus, who is there who does not know that the city of the Ephesians is the temple keeper of the great Artemis." ᴱˢⱽ **18:35**

There was no need for their chants. He went on to say Gaius and Aristarchus were not robbers or blasphemers of the goddess. He reminded them that if they had a complaint against any man, the courts of law were open for them to plead their case in a lawful assembly. And he concluded:

"For we really are in danger of being charged with rioting today, since there is no cause that we can give to justify this commotion." And when he had said these things, he dismissed the assembly. ᴱˢⱽ **19:40-41**

Paul came close to losing his life at Ephesus. He wrote of the trouble he had experienced in Ephesus, saying, "We despaired even of life. But we had the sentence of death in ourselves **that we should not trust in ourselves but in God** who raises the dead; who delivered us from so great a death." (2 Cor. 1:8-10)

NOTES

The Conclusion of the Journey
Acts 20

And after the uproar was ceased, Paul called to him the disciples, and embraced them, and departed for to go into Macedonia. 20:1

Because of the uproar caused by the silversmiths, Paul decided to leave Ephesus earlier than he had planned. He called the brethren together to encourage them and bid them farewell. Then he departed for Macedonia by way of Troas, where he had received the Macedonian call on his second missionary journey. (16:8-9)

He had sent Titus to Corinth to see if they had repented of their sins that are mentioned in 1 Corinthians. Paul was expecting to meet Titus at Troas with news from Corinth. Later he wrote, "When I came to Troas to preach Christ's gospel, and a door was opened to me of the Lord, I had no rest in my spirit, because I found not Titus my brother; but taking my leave of them, I went into Macedonia." (2 Cor. 2:12-13) As Paul waited for Titus in Troas, he was given the opportunity to preach the gospel with success, but desiring to hear from Titus, he went on to Philippi, his first stop in Macedonia. But Titus was not there. Paul wrote, "When we were come into Macedonia, our flesh had no rest." (2 Cor. 7:5) Titus soon arrived at either Philippi or Thessalonica with good news, along with some bad, which caused Paul to write 2 Corinthians.

And when he had gone over those parts and had given them much exhortation, he came into Greece, and abode there three months. 20:2-3

As Paul traveled through Philippi, Thessalonica and Berea, he exhorted the brethren; and when he came to Corinth, he wrote his letter to the Romans.

And when the Jews laid wait for him as he was about to sail into Syria, he purposed to return through Macedonia. 20:3

Having finished the collection for the poor saints in Jerusalem, Paul's original plan was to sail for Syria from Corinth's seaport at Cenchrea. But a plot against Paul by the Jews was discovered there. Not only was Paul's life in jeopardy but also the contribution to the saints. So, Paul decided to return over land through Macedonia.

And he was accompanied by Sopater of Berea, the son of Pyrrhus; and by Aristarchus and Secundus of the Thessalonians; and Gaius of Derbe, and Timothy; and Tychicus and Trophimus of Asia. But these had gone on ahead and waiting for us at Troas. NASB **20:4-5**

These seven men were going to Jerusalem with the contribution for the saints. In 2 Corinthians 8:19, Paul mentions an unnamed brother "who was also chosen by the churches to travel with us with this gift." NKJV This may be a reference to Luke. Paul told the Corinthians these precautions were taken so "that no man should blame us in this abundance which is administrated by us; providing for honest things, not only in the sight of the Lord, but also in the sight of men." (2 Cor. 8:20)

And we sailed away from Philippi after the days of unleavened bread, and came to them to Troas in five days; where we abode seven days. 20:6

Luke joined Paul at Philippi; he is saying "we" again. Those bearing the charitable gift went on to Troas and waited for Paul and Luke, who remained at Philippi until after the Passover. Arriving at Troas, they stayed there for seven days. Several times in his travels, Paul stayed seven days in cities in order to be with his brethren on Sunday, the Lord's Day. (21:4; 28:14)

And upon the first day of the week, when the disciples came together to break bread, Paul preached to them, ready to depart on the morrow, and continued his speech until midnight. 20:7

Churches were meeting together "**on the first day of every week.**" NASB (1 Cor. 16:1-2) The word translated **every** is in the Greek text. Their purpose of their meeting together is given in Acts 20:7 – "the disciples came together to break bread." Christians had observed the Lord's Supper since the day of Pentecost. (Acts 2:42) Paul wrote, "The cup of blessing which we bless, is it not the communion of the blood of Christ? The bread which we break, is it not the communion of the body of Christ?" (1 Cor. 10:16) Christians met on the first day of every week to remember Christ's death, burial, and resurrection. (1 Cor. 11:23-25) Their reason for meeting on Sundays was to share in the Lord's Supper.

And there were many lights in the upper chamber where they were gathered together. 20:8

Since Troas was a Roman colony, the church would be using the Roman method of counting time, not Jewish. Reese says, "If we accept the idea that this was a night meeting, there is a ready explanation for the time of the services. Slaves in the service of heathen masters would have to meet for worship very late in the day, after their labors were finished." [62]

---

[62] Gareth L. Reese, *New Testament History—Acts,* p. 734

There sat in a window a certain young man named Eutychus, being fallen into a deep sleep. And as Paul was long in preaching, he sunk down in sleep and fell from the third floor, and was taken up dead. 20:9

Eutychus is described as a young man in verse 9 and as a boy in verse 12; he was probably in his late teens. The windows were openings in the wall with shutters, but the shutters were open to let fresh air into the large room. Eutychus may have been sitting in a window due to the crowd or to feel a breeze after working all day. As Paul continued preaching, Eutychus fell into a deep sleep and fell out the window from the third floor. He "was taken up dead." He was not taken up **as** dead; he was taken up dead.

Paul went down, and fell on him, and embracing him said, "Trouble not yourselves; for his life is in him." 20:10

Life had returned to Eutychus. This was an impressive miracle. The fall must have broken bones, dislocated joints, torn ligaments, injured organs besides stopping his heart beat. But through the power of the Holy Spirit, he was fully restored. Peter raised Tabitha from the dead; Paul raised Eutychus from the dead.

When he therefore was come up again and had broken bread and eaten, and talked a long while, even till break of day, so he departed. 20:11

Paul's breaking of bread refers to a common meal that he needed for refreshment. Paul thought this could be his last visit with the brethren in Troas (cf. 20:38), so he stayed up all night with them. They observed the Lord's Supper when they came together. Surely the elderly and many others could not stay up past midnight like Paul did. Compare the breaking of bread in Acts 2:42 with that in Acts 2:46.

The Conclusion of the Journey | 165

And they took away the boy alive, and were greatly comforted. NASB **20:12**

They returned the boy to his home alive, instead of dead. The resurrection of the dead was a proven fact! This was a great comfort to all at Troas.

We went on ahead to the ship and sailed for Assos, where we were going to take Paul aboard. He had made this arrangement because he was going there on foot. When he met us at Assos, we took him aboard and went on to Mitylene. The next day we set sail from there and arrived off Kios. The day after that we crossed over to Samos, and on the following day arrived at Miletus. Paul had decided to sail past Ephesus to avoid spending time in the province of Asia, for he was in a hurry to reach Jerusalem, if possible, by the day of Pentecost. From Miletus, Paul sent to Ephesus for the elders. NIV **20:13-17**

From Troas, Luke and the others sailed to Assos, while Paul walked twenty miles to join them there. Paul may have continued visiting with some of the brethren as he walked. He boarded the ship at Assos; and four days later they arrived at Miletus, a seaport thirty miles from Ephesus.

Paul did not have time to go to Ephesus, because he desired to be in Jerusalem by the day of Pentecost. So, he asked the elders of the church to meet him at Miletus for a brief visit, while his ship was anchored for three or four days to unload and to load cargo. Since over a year had passed since his departure from Ephesus, Paul wanted to encourage these men who had oversight of the church. Notice: Paul did not send for the pastor or for the bishop, but for the elders, plural in number.

And when they had come to him, he said to them, "You know, from the first day I came to Asia, in what

manner I always lived among you, serving the Lord with all humility, with many tears and trials which happened to me by the plotting of the Jews." NKJV 20:18-19**

Paul is reminding the elders of how he had lived among them to encourage them to follow Christ. False teachers already were perverting the gospel and troubling Christians in Galatia (Galatians 1:6-9) and also at Corinth (2 Cor.11:2-4). They needed to follow Paul's example of serving the Lord with humility and tears of concern for the lost and fallen. Paul had endured trials by the Jews at Ephesus. Paul was saying to the elders, "Be ye followers of me, even as I also am of Christ." (1 Cor. 11:1)

"I kept back nothing that was profitable to you, but have shown you and taught you publicly and from house to house, testifying both to the Jews and also to the Greeks, repentance toward God and faith toward our Lord Jesus Christ." 20:20-21

Paul had taught them publicly in the synagogue and in the school of Tyrannus and privately from house to house, explaining all things that were profitable for them. Both Jews and Greeks needed to repent and turn to the one true God in order to have faith toward our Lord Jesus Christ. The Jews misunderstood the prophecies concerning the Messiah and the kingdom of God, and the Greeks needed to turn from their idols to serve the true and living God.

"And now, behold, I go bound in the spirit to Jerusalem, not knowing the things that shall befall me there; save that the Holy Spirit witnesses in every city, saying that bonds and afflictions await me." 20:22-23

Some translations have "Spirit," referring to the Holy Spirit; other translations have "spirit," speaking of Paul's spirit. Roper says, "The meaning is basically the same whether a small "s" or a capital "S" is used: Paul had "purposed in [his] spirit to go to Jerusalem" (19:21), no doubt because he was convinced it was God's will." [63]

"But none of these things move me; nor do I count my life dear to myself, so that I might finish my race with joy, and the ministry which I have received of the Lord Jesus to testify to the gospel of the grace of God." NKJV **20:24**

Paul would not be moved by fear of suffering even death, because the Lord Jesus had given him the ministry of preaching the gospel of God's grace to the Gentiles and to Israel. (Acts 9:15) Paul was dedicated to preaching the good news of God's grace, because he knew that he had received God's grace. (1 Cor. 15:10) His mind was fixed on staying on his course and finishing his race with joy, and he did. (2 Tim. 4:6-8) He left us a great example.

"And now, behold, I know that you all, among whom I have gone preaching the kingdom of God, shall see my face no more." 20:25

Paul was ready to die at Jerusalem. (21:13) However, Paul admitted in verse 22 that he did not know what would happen to him in Jerusalem; he only knew that the Holy Spirit had revealed "that bonds and afflictions awaited" him there. (v. 23) If he was spared death, his plans were to go to Rome and then to Spain. (Romans 16:22-25) Paul thought he would not see them again. But after his first imprisonment at Rome, it seems that he did go to Ephesus. (1 Timothy 1:3; 3:14; 4:13) Some of the elders may have died before Paul's return, so he did not see all of their faces again.

"Therefore, I declare to you today that I am innocent of the blood of all men. For I have not hesitated to proclaim to you the whole will of God." NIV **20:26-27**

---

[63] David L. Roper, Ibid., p. 243

Paul had made known to them everything God wants us to do. If any were lost, Paul was not responsible.

"Therefore, take heed to yourselves and all the flock, among which the Holy Spirit has made you overseers, to shepherd the church of God, which he purchased with his own blood." NKJV **20:28**

Elders first must be on guard for themselves. They are to give attention to their own faith and life. They could be tempted with sinful pride, causing them to insist on their own way instead of God's way. They are to be examples to the believers, not lords. (1 Peter 5:3) Secondly, they are to guard the members of the church like good shepherds. The Holy Spirit had made them overseers by providing the qualifications for elders. They are to take care of the members and feed them with the word of God. They have the oversight of the work of the church, which was purchased by the blood of Christ. The church of God is the church of Christ, because He is the divine One who shed his own blood. The word "bishop" is the Anglicized form of the Greek word for "overseer." The elders of the church in Ephesus were also called "overseers" (bishops) and shepherds (pastors). Elder, bishop and pastor refer to the same office, and there was always a plural number in each congregation. There was never a single pastor or a bishop over a church or over a number of churches.

"For I know this: that after my departure savage wolves will come in among you, not sparing the flock. Also, from among yourselves men will rise up, speaking perverse things, to draw away disciples after themselves." NKJV **20:29**

Jesus compared false teachers to wolves in Matthew 7:15. Timothy was at Ephesus when Paul wrote that some had made shipwreck of the faith. (1 Timothy 1:3-20) Jesus praised the church at Ephesus because they had exposed the false apostles, including the Nicolaitans, but he rebuked them for leaving their first love. (Rev. 2:1-6)

"Therefore, watch and remember that by the space of three years I ceased not to warn everyone night and day with tears." 20:31

Because of the dangers facing the church, the elders needed to be alert. Paul had set the example for them to follow during the three years he was with them.

"And now, brethren, I commend you to God and to the word of his grace, which is able to build you up and to give you an inheritance among all those who are sanctified." 20:32

Paul was entrusting their care and protection to God and to his word. Faith should not be in men but in God. And saving faith comes from hearing the word of God. (Romans 10:17) God's word is able to strengthen us and give us an inheritance in heaven. Besides their hearing the gospel of Christ, Paul already had written the books of Galatians, 1 & 2 Thessalonians, 1 & 2 Corinthians, and Romans. Already in circulation or soon to be written was the gospel according to Mark. [64] Paul concluded his message with these words:

"I have coveted no man's silver, or gold, or apparel. Yes, you yourselves know that these hands have ministered to my necessities and to them that were with me. I have shown you all things, how that so laboring you ought to support the weak, and to remember the words of the Lord, how he said, 'It is more blessed to give than to receive.'" 20:33-35

Being a preacher or elder in Christ's church should not be a means of gaining material wealth. An elder must be "free

---

[64] Bruce Wilkinson & Kenneth Boa, *Talk Thru the Bible,* p. 319

from the love of money." (1 Tim. 3:3; Titus 1:7) Paul had worked among the rich, but he did not desire their money or their clothes. Paul had the right to be supported financially (1 Cor. 9:9-18), but he did not use that right. He made tents with his hands to support his needs. Jesus had taught him by his example and by words, "It is more blessed to give than to receive."

And when he had thus spoken, he knelt down and prayed with them all. And they all wept aloud and fell on Paul's neck and kissed him, sorrowing most of all for the words which he spoke, that they should see his face no more. And they accompanied him to the ship. 20:36-38

This was an emotional scene. Paul knelt in prayer for God's guidance and protection to be with them. Being very close to Paul and believing that they would not see him again caused them to weep aloud. The kiss was the standard form of farewell as well as a greeting. They went with Paul all the way to the ship.

The Journey to Jerusalem
Acts 21

Paul and his company sailed from Miletus to **the island of Cos**, the home of Hippocrates (c. 460-377 BC), who founded the world's most famous medical school. Physicians today still take the Hippocratic Oath. **21:1**

The next day they came to **the island of Rhodes**, where one of the Seven Wonders of the Ancient World once stood—the 105-foot-high bronze statue of Colossus at its harbor. An earthquake had broken the statue by the time of Paul's visit, but its ruins were still there. From Rhodes they sailed to the port of **Patara** on the mainland of Asia Minor. There they found a ship going straight to Phoenicia. **21:1-2**

As they sailed past **the island of Cyprus** to the left side of the ship, Paul could see where he began his first missionary journey. They landed at **Tyre** for the ship to unload its cargo. The city of Tyre was a Roman colony and the major seaport of Phoenicia. **21:3**

And finding disciples, we stayed there seven days. They told Paul through the Spirit that he should not go up to Jerusalem. NKJV **21:4**

Paul and his men were able to worship with the church at Tyre on the Lord's Day at least once during a stay of seven days. These disciples were warning Paul not to go to Jerusalem, because the Spirit had revealed to them, as he had in other places, that afflictions and bonds awaited him there. All the brethren including the women and children went with Paul and his companions to the shore, where they knelt down and prayed. Luke writes, **"After saying good-by to each other, we went aboard the ship, and they returned home. 21:5-6**

And when we had finished our voyage from Tyre, we came to Ptolemais, and greeted the brethren, and stayed with them one day. 21:7

Ptolemais was about 30 miles south of Tyre. The city was once known as "Acco" in Judges 1:31. After the death of Alexander the Great, the city was named for the Ptolemy kings of Egypt. Paul had a brief visit with the brethren at this Roman colony.

And on the next day we departed and came to Caesarea; and entering the house of Philip the evangelist, who was one of the seven, we stayed with him. Now this man had four virgin daughters, who were prophetesses. NASB **21:8-9**

The city of Caesarea was about 35 miles south of Ptolemais. Philip was one of the seven men appointed to serve tables in Acts 6:2-6. He was also the evangelist who made many converts in the city of Samaria and baptized the Ethiopian eunuch in Acts 8. Then traveling along the coast of the Mediterranean Sea, Philip preached in all the cities until he came to Caesarea, where he made it his home. (Acts 8:40)

After Paul's first visit with the apostles in Jerusalem, he went to Caesarea on his way back to Tarsus. (Acts 9:26-30) And after his second missionary journey Paul landed at Caesarea on his way to Jerusalem and Antioch. (Acts 18:22) During these times at Caesarea, Paul probably became well acquainted with Philip. He is called the evangelist to distinguish him from Philip the apostle. His four daughters had the gift of prophesy, fulfilling Joel's prophecy, which was quoted by Peter in Acts 2:17 on the day of Pentecost. Women used this gift in a private setting, but not in a public worship assembly. (1 Cor. 14:23, 31-37). The words of many of our best hymns have been written by women. It appears that Philip's daughters remained virgins in order to give themselves completely to the Lord's service. (1 Cor. 7:34-35)

And as we stayed many days, a certain prophet named Agabus came down from Judea. When he had come to us, he took Paul's belt and bound his own hands and feet, and said, "Thus says the Holy Spirit, 'So shall the Jews at Jerusalem bind the man that owns this belt and shall deliver him into the hands of the Gentiles.'" NKJV **21:10-11**

Paul's days with Philip may have strengthened him, both physically and spiritually. However, his rest was interrupted by Agabus, a prophet from Jerusalem. He was the prophet who had predicted the famine during the time of Claudius Caesar. (Acts 11:28) Like the prophets of old, Agabus acted out his prophecy. The Holy Spirit was saying that Paul would be bound by the Jews at Jerusalem and given to the Roman authorities.

Now when we heard these things, both we and those from that place pleaded with him not to go up to Jerusalem. Then Paul answered, "What do you mean by weeping and breaking my heart? For I am ready not only to be bound, but also to die at Jerusalem for the name of the Lord Jesus." So when he would not be persuaded, we ceased, saying, "The will of the Lord be done." NKJV **21:12-14**

Luke and his fellow-travelers, along with the brethren at Caesarea, began begging Paul not to go to Jerusalem. But Paul was ready to die at Jerusalem. He felt obligated to go to Jerusalem with the gift that he had promised for the poor. (Gal. 2:10) Also, the Lord had told Paul that he would bear Christ's name before the Gentiles and kings. (Acts 9:15) It was the Lord's will for Paul to be arrested in order to preach to governors and kings.

After these days we got ready and started on our way up to Jerusalem. And some of the disciples from Caesarea also came with us, taking us to Mnason of Cyprus, a disciple of long standing with whom we were to lodge. NASB **21:15-16**

Brethren from Caesarea went with Paul's group on their sixty-five-mile journey to Jerusalem. Mnason was from the island of Cyprus, but he now lived in Jerusalem in a house big enough to accommodate Paul and his fellow travelers. He had been a Christian for a long time and was probably known for his hospitality.

And when we were come to Jerusalem, the brethren received us gladly. And the day following, Paul went in with us to James; and all the elders were present. And when he had greeted them, he declared particularly what things God had done among the Gentiles by his ministry. And when they heard it, they glorified the Lord. 21:17-20

The day after their arriving in Jerusalem, Paul and his associates met with James and the elders to deliver the contribution for the poor. Paul reported what God had accomplished during his third missionary journey, and the brethren began praising God.

And they said to him, "You see, brother, how many thousands there are among the Jews of those who have believed. They are all zealous for the law, and they have been told about you that you are teaching all the Jews who are among the Gentiles to forsake Moses, telling them not to circumcise their children or walk according to our customs." ESV **21:20-21**

These elders pointed out to Paul that there were thousands of Jewish Christians who, due to conscience, were still observing the Sabbath, avoiding unclean meats, and other things in the law of Moses. Paul had already written: "One man regards one day above another; another regards every day alike. Let each man be fully convinced in his own mind. He who observes the day, observes it for the Lord, and he who eats, does so for the Lord, for he gives thanks to God; and he who eats not, for the Lord he does not eat, and gives thanks to God. For the kingdom of God is not meat and drink, but righteousness and peace and joy in the Holy Spirit." ᴺᴬˢᴮ (Rom. 14:5-6, 17) Paul believed it was right for a Jew to observe the Sabbath and other things under the law in personal devotion to God, but he would not allow the binding of the law on the Gentiles.

"What then is to be done? They will certainly hear that you have come. Do therefore what we tell you. We have four men who are under a vow; take these men and purify yourself along with them and pay their expenses, so that they may shave their heads. Thus all will know that there is nothing in what they have been told about you, but that you yourself also live in observance of the law. But as for the Gentiles who have believed, we have sent a letter with our judgment that they should abstain from what has been sacrificed to idols, and from blood, and from what has been strangled, and from sexual immorality." ᴱˢⱽ **21:22-25**

Some of the Jewish Christians were misrepresenting Paul. Actions speak louder than words. If Paul would take part in the purification of these four men, everyone would know that the charges against Paul were false. Paul had shown in his own life that he himself observed Jewish traditions, but he would not bind them on others. Toward the end of his second journey, Paul shaved his head at Cenchrea, because he had taken a vow. (Acts 18:18) He was showing his thanksgiving and devotion to God in Jewish tradition. The Jerusalem elders stated, as they had before, that the Gentiles should not be required to observe the law of Moses.

Then Paul took the men, and the next day, purifying himself with them entered into the temple to signify the accomplishment of the days of purification, until that an offering should be offered for every one of them. 21:26

Paul and the four men washed their bodies and put on clean clothes to begin their purification. Roper explains, "The four men would not be allowed to enter the temple until their seven-day purification was completed, but Paul's ceremonial cleansing would take only a day or so. (Leviticus 15:1-30) He could go into the temple on their behalf, making arrangements for the sacrifices to be offered at the end of their days of purification." [65] Paul had written in 1 Corinthians 9:20, "And unto the Jews I became a Jew, that I might gain the Jews." Paul would not offend their consciences. (Romans 14:21-23)

And when the seven days were almost ended, the Jews which were of Asia, when they saw him in the temple, stirred up all the people and laid hands on him, crying out, "Men of Israel, help! This is the man that teaches all men everywhere against the people and the law and this place; and furthermore, brought Greeks also into the temple and has polluted this holy place." (For they had seen before with him in the city Trophimus an Ephesian, whom they supposed that Paul had brought into the temple.) 21:27-29

Before the four men had completed their purification, some Jews from the Roman province of Asia started a riot against Paul. These accusers, who were probably from Ephesus, recognized Trophimus with Paul in the city. When they saw Paul entering the temple, they accused him of having brought Gentiles into the temple and polluting it.

---

[65] David L. Roper, *Truth for Today Commentary, Acts 15-28*, p. 290

They may have assumed the four men seeking purification were also Gentiles. The punishment for bringing a Gentile past the Court of the Gentiles into the inner courts was death. These Jews also accused Paul of teaching against the Jewish people, their law, and the temple. The Jews had used false accusations before against Jesus and Stephen.

And all the city was moved, and the people ran together; and they took Paul and drew him out of the temple, and immediately the doors were shut. 21:30

Paul was dragged out of the temple so his blood would not pollute it. The doors to the temple may have been shut so that the worshipers would not be disturbed. Some see the shutting of the temple doors as being symbolic of the future destruction of the temple in AD 70.

And as they went about to kill him, a report came to the chief captain of the cohort that all Jerusalem was in an uproar. He immediately took soldiers and centurions and ran down to them. And when they saw the chief captain and the soldiers, they left off beating Paul. 21:32 This is the second time Roman authorities delivered Paul from the Jews. (cf. 18:12-16)

Then the chief captain came near, and took him, and commanded him to be bound with two chains; and demanded who he was and what he had done. And some cried one thing, some another, among the crowd. And when he could not know the certainty for the tumult, he commanded him to be carried into the fortress. 21:34

The chief captain was over a cohort of at least 600 men. We learn from Acts 23:22-26, that his name was Claudius Lysias. His job was to quiet the mob. So, he had Paul bound with two chains, likely between two soldiers, as was Peter (12:6). When he could not find out the cause of the disturbance, he ordered Paul to be carried to the Fortress Antonia, located at the northwest corner of the temple area. This fortress had watch towers overlooking the temple.

When he got to the stairs, it so happened that he was carried by the soldiers because of the violence of the mob; for the multitude of the people kept following behind, crying out, "Away with him!" NASB **21:35-36**

Paul had to be carried by the soldiers, lifting him up above the angry mob that was demanding his death.

And as Paul was about to be brought into the barracks, he said to the commander, "May I say something to you?" And he said, "Do you know Greek? Then you are not the Egyptian who some time ago stirred up a revolt and led the four thousand men of the Assassins out into the wilderness?" But Paul said, "I am a Jew of Tarsus in Cilicia, a citizen of no insignificant city; and I beg you, allow me to speak to the people." NASB **21:37-39**

Although Paul had been beaten, he wanted to testify of God's grace. He had stated this desire in Acts 20:24. At first, the commander thought Paul was a notorious Egyptian troublemaker. He was surprised when Paul spoke Greek, and then he knew he was not the Egyptian. After Paul identified himself as a Jew from the city of Tarsus, he was given permission to speak to the mob.

Paul's Defense before a Mob
Acts 22

Roman soldiers rescued Paul from an angry Jewish mob at the temple in Jerusalem. As they were about to enter the Fortress Antonia, Paul asked the chief captain for permission to speak to the people, and he granted it.

Paul, standing on the stairs, motioned to the people with his hand; and when there was made a great hush, he spoke to them in the Hebrew dialect, saying, "Brethren and fathers, hear my defense which I now offer to you." And when they heard that he was addressing them in the Hebrew dialect, they became even more quiet. NASB **21:40 – 22:2**

Paul stood on the stairs, beaten and bruised. He motioned with his hand, showing that he wanted their attention. The crowd began to quiet down, perhaps out of curiosity as to who he was. Paul began speaking to them in Hebrew. He called them brethren, identifying himself as a member of the Jewish family, and he called the older men fathers out of respect. His speaking in Hebrew assured them that he was a Jew. So, they listened even more quietly. And Paul said,

"I am a Jew, born in Tarsus of Cilicia, but brought up in this city, educated under Gamaliel, strictly according to the law of our fathers, and zealous for God, just as you all are today." NASB **22:3**

Many in the crowd did not know him, because it had been twenty years since he had lived in Jerusalem. Paul wanted the Jews to know that he was a Jew, who had been brought up in Jerusalem and educated under Gamaliel, a greatly respected rabbi. As a Jew, Paul understood their zeal for God's law.

"And I persecuted this way unto the death, binding and delivering into prisons both men and women." 22:4

Paul's zeal toward God and the Law had caused him to persecute "this way," the followers of Jesus, just as his audience was seeking his death. He had already written, "I bear them record that they have a zeal of God, but not according to knowledge." (Romans 10:2)

"As also the high priest bears me witness, and all the council of the elders, from whom also I received letters to the brethren, and went to Damascus to bring them who were there bound to Jerusalem for to be punished." 22:5

The high priest and the Sanhedrin were witnesses to Paul's zeal for the Jewish faith. They had given Paul letters of authority to arrest the followers of Jesus in Damascus and bring them to Jerusalem for punishment. Paul now explains to his audience how he went from being one who zealously persecuted Christians to being a preacher of the gospel of Jesus Christ to the Gentiles.

"And it came to pass, that as I made my journey and was come near to Damascus about noon, suddenly there shone from heaven a great light round about me. And I fell to the ground and heard a voice saying to me, 'Saul, Saul, why are you persecuting me?' And I answered, 'Who are you, Lord?' And he said to me, 'I am Jesus of Nazareth, whom you are persecuting.'" 22:6-8

Paul's trip to Damascus to persecute Christians was interrupted by a bright light from heaven. It was brighter than the sun at noon, and it caused Paul to fall to the ground. Paul heard a voice calling him by his Hebrew name, "Saul, Saul, why are you persecuting me?" This voice was coming from heaven, so he asked, "Who are you, Lord?" Paul was surprised when he heard, "I am Jesus of Nazareth, whom you are persecuting." Jesus is alive in heaven! Jesus was not a blasphemer. He was indeed the Son of God in the flesh.

"And they that were with me saw indeed the light, and were afraid; but they heard not the voice of him that spoke to me." 22:9

Luke's account says those traveling with Saul were hearing the sound of the voice (Acts 9:7; *akouo* with the genitive), but Paul tells us that they did not understand it. (*akouo* with the accusative; cf. 1 Corinthians 14:2) Those journeying with Paul were witnesses to the light and the sound, which caused them to be afraid.

"And I said, 'What shall I do, Lord?' And the Lord said to me, 'Arise, and go into Damascus, and there it shall be told you of all things which are appointed for you to do.'" 22:10

Paul now recognized Jesus as divine, and he was ready to obey him. Jesus would use a disciple to tell him what to do. We are reminded again that the treasure of Christ's gospel is in men, "earthen vessels." (2 Cor. 4:3-7)

"And when I could not see for the glory of that light, being led by the hand of them that were with me, I came into Damascus." 22:11

Paul was the only one that was blinded by the light. Roper observes, "Saul had expected to sweep into Damascus with a show of strength as God's avenging agent; instead, he was led into the city a sorrowing sinner, as helpless as a blind beggar." [66] For Luke's account of the conversion of Saul, see Acts 9:8-21.

"And one Ananias, a devout man according to the law, having a good report of all the Jews, which dwelt there, came to me, and stood, and said to me, 'Brother

---

[66] David L. Roper, *Truth for Today Commentary, Acts 1-14*, p. 331

Saul, receive your sight.' And the same hour I looked up at him." 22:12-13

Ananias calls Saul "brother" because they were both of the Jewish family. First, Ananias restored Paul's sight. This miracle was a sign to Paul that Ananias would be the one who would tell him what the Lord wanted him to do. And Ananias said to Paul,

"The God of our fathers has chosen you that you should know His will, and see the Just One, and hear the voice of His mouth. For you will be His witness to all men of what you have seen and heard. And now why are you waiting? Arise and be baptized, and wash away your sins, calling on the name of the Lord." NKJV 22:14-16

God had chosen Paul to know his will and see Jesus Christ, the Just One, and to hear the voice of Jesus. Paul wrote that "it pleased God ... to reveal his Son in me, that I might preach him." (Galatians 1:15-16) The gospel that Paul preached was "by the revelation of Jesus Christ." (Galatians 1:11-12) Paul testified that he had seen Jesus after his death and resurrection. (1 Cor. 15:3-8)

When Paul saw Jesus, he realized his terrible guilt in persecuting Christ and his church. He thought of himself as the chief of sinners. (1 Timothy 1:15-16) He asked the Lord, "What shall I do?" The Lord told him to go into the city and it would be told him what to do. Paul was so concerned about his condition that he would not eat or drink for three days as he was praying. (Acts 9:9, 11) And now, Ananias told Paul what to do. **"Arise and be baptized and wash away your sins calling on the name of the Lord."** (22:16)

After three days of believing in Jesus and praying, Paul still had his sins. These sins would be washed away by the blood of Jesus (Rev. 1:5) **when** he was immersed in water, calling on the name of the Lord. Paul is telling us how he called upon the name of the Lord for salvation. (Romans 10:13)

"And it came to pass, that, when I was come again to Jerusalem, even while I prayed in the temple, I was in a trance and saw him saying to me, 'Make haste and get quickly out of Jerusalem for they will not receive your testimony concerning me.' And I said, 'Lord, they know that I imprisoned and beat in every synagogue those who believed on you. And when the blood of your martyr Stephen was shed, I also was standing by, and consenting to his death, and kept the clothes of those who slew him.' And he said to me, 'Depart, for I will send you far from here to the Gentiles.'" 22:17-21

Paul's visit to Jerusalem came three years after his conversion. (Galatians 1:15-18) During this fifteen-day visit, Paul disputed with the Greek speaking Jews, his former associates, hoping to convert them to Christ. (Acts 9:26-30), but they attempted to kill him. Jesus warned Paul that they would not hear him and that he should get out of Jerusalem. Jesus was sending him to the Gentiles.

And they gave him audience unto this word, and then they lifted up their voices and said, "Away with such a fellow from the earth, for it is not fit that he should live." 22:22

The word "Gentiles" inflamed their prejudices and reminded them that Paul was accused of bringing Gentiles into the temple. They were calling for Paul to die. Their intolerance and prejudice kept them from hearing the rest of Paul's message — the good news that in Christ all the nations of the earth shall be blessed in fulfillment of the promise made to their fathers. (Genesis 22:18)

And as they cried out and cast off their clothes and threw dust into the air, the chief captain commanded him to be brought into the fortress and said that he should be examined by scourging; that he might know why they cried so against him. 22:24

The crowd was out of control. The throwing of dust into the air was a sign of condemnation, and perhaps their taking off their outer clothes was showing their desire to stone him. (7:58) This caused the chief captain to bring Paul inside the fortress. To find out why the crowd was so against Paul, he said that Paul should be examined by scourging. A *scourge* was four or five strips of leather attached to a wooden handle. Imbedded in the leather strips were bits of bone and metal that would rip the flesh with every lash. It was a very cruel form of punishment.

And as they bound him with thongs, Paul said to the centurion that stood by, "Is it lawful for you to scourge a man who is a Roman and uncondemned?" 22:25

As they were stretching Paul's body over a whipping post, tying him down with strips of leather, he revealed his Roman citizenship to the centurion that was in charge of the scourging. It was against Roman law to bind and scourge a Roman citizen without his being found guilty by a trial. Being a Roman citizen, Paul knew his rights; and the centurion knew the law.

When the centurion heard that, he went and told the chief captain, saying, "Take care what you do for this man is a Roman." Then the chief captain came and said to him, "Tell me, are you a Roman?"

He said, "Yes." 22:26-27

Wade writes, "Paul's reply that he was a Roman citizen removed some of the commander's skepticism. Of course,

Paul could have been lying in order to escape a beating. But while Paul did not carry around with him proof of his citizenship, his claim could readily be checked against the citizenship list of Tarsus. A prisoner was not likely to make a false claim, for this was punishable by death." [67]

The commander answered, "With a large sum I obtained this citizenship." And Paul said, "But I was born a citizen." NKJV **22:28**

Roper explains Roman citizenship: "Legally, Roman citizenship was acquired by being born in Rome or a Roman colony, or by having citizenship bestowed by the government for unusual service rendered. It could also be acquired illegally by bribing officials, which is evidently what the commander had done." [68] The chief captain was probably thinking, "How could this beaten-up Jew come up with enough money to bribe a Roman official?" But Paul answered, "I was born a Roman citizen."

Then immediately those who were about to examine him withdrew from him; and the commander was also afraid after he found out that he was a Roman, and because he had bound him. The next day, because he wanted to know for certain why he was accused by the Jews, he released him from his bonds, and commanded the chief priests and all their council to appear, and brought Paul down and set him before them. NKJV **22:29-30**

It was against Roman law even **to bind** a Roman citizen. This explains why the commander later stretched the truth in his letter to governor Felix in Acts 23:26-30. Either Paul's chains were removed, or he was removed from his cell. Paul was now in protective custody. The next day, Paul was brought before the Sanhedrin, the highest council of the

---

[67] John W. Wade, *Acts*, p. 236
[68] David L. Roper, *Truth for Today Commentary, Acts 15-28*, p. 326

Jews, so the commander could know for certain their accusation against Paul.

The Plot against Paul
Acts 23

In order to find out the accusation that the Jews had against Paul, the chief captain Claudius Lysias brought Paul before the chief priests and the Sanhedrin. (22:30)

And Paul, earnestly beholding the council, said, "Men and brethren, I have lived in all good conscience before God until this day." 23:1

Paul was looking intently at the Sanhedrin. Perhaps he knew some of them. Nearly twenty-five years earlier, this council had given him letters of authority to bind disciples of Jesus in Damascus. Paul wanted the council to know that he was sincerely trying to do right and serve God as he always had done. Paul had been zealous in persecuting Christians while thinking he "ought to do many things contrary to the name of Jesus of Nazareth." (26:9) However, this same good conscience had caused Paul to believe in Jesus and to be zealous in preaching the gospel after Jesus appeared to him with the truth. A good conscience causes one to do what he believes is right. We should never go against our conscience (Romans 14:23), but we should always have an open mind to the truth.

And the high priest Ananias commanded them that stood by him to smite him on the mouth.

Roper writes, "It was easier for the high priest to strike Paul than to answer him—for the high priest had no provable accusation to bring against him." [69] The Jewish historian Josephus said that this Ananias was one of the most unscrupulous men ever to be high priest. He stole tithes from his own priests and had people murdered so

---

[69] David L. Roper, *Truth for Today Commentary, Acts 15-28*, p. 342

he could stay in power. [70] He had not lived in all good conscience as Paul had. He may have thought that Paul was exposing him. Ananias the high priest should not be confused with "Annas the high priest" in Acts 4:6.

Then Paul said to him, "God shall smite you, you whited wall, for do you sit to judge me after the law and command me to be smitten contrary to the law?" 23:3

By calling Ananias a "whited wall" Paul was accusing him of being a hypocrite, just as Jesus condemned the Pharisees for being "whited sepulchers" in Matthew 23:27. Ananias as a judge had broken the Law by having Paul struck on the mouth, for the Law stated that no one was to be punished until he had been tried and found guilty. (Deuteronomy 25:1, 2) Paul knew the Law; he had been taught by the famous rabbi Gamaliel.

And they that stood by said, "Do you revile God's high priest?" Then Paul said, "I knew not, brethren, that he was the high priest; for it is written, 'You shall not speak evil of the ruler of your people.'" 23:4-5

Some commentaries think that Paul was apologizing for his rebuke of the high priest. Others believe Paul was not taking back anything that he said. Ananias was a wicked man who had usurped the office of high priest by bribery and corruption. Paul did not recognize him as the rightful high priest. The Holy Spirit was speaking through Paul when he said to Ananias, "God shall smite you, you whited wall." Just eight years later in AD 66, patriotic Jews assassinated Ananias for collaborating with the Romans.[71] God smote him! Paul's words were true. He was justifying what he had said. If Ananias had been

---

[70] Josephus, *Antiquities,* 20.9.2, 4
[71] Josephus, *Wars* 2.17.9

a rightful high priest, judging according to the Law, Paul would not have spoken against him. The prophets spoke against their wicked rulers. Isaiah condemned the rulers of God's people in the time of king Ahaz. He called them "rulers of Sodom." He said they were "rebellious and companions of thieves; everyone loves bribes." (Isaiah 1:10, 23) These words also could be used to describe Ananias. Wade writes, "We need to realize that Paul was not concerned at that moment in defending himself. He was quite willing to suffer and die for his faith if necessary. He was, rather, defending a principle. His concern was that the gospel would get a fair and honest hearing, a hearing that would not be prejudiced by the arrogant actions of the high priest. As a defender of the faith, Paul had every right to challenge the illegal actions of Ananias." [72] However, we should honor and respect our rightful rulers.

But when Paul perceived that the one part were Sadducees, and the other Pharisees, he cried out in the council, "Men and brethren, I am a Pharisee, the son of a Pharisee. Of the hope and resurrection of the dead I am called in question." And when he had so said, there arose a dissension between the Pharisees and the Sadducees; and the assembly was divided. For the Sadducees say that there is no resurrection, neither angel, nor spirit; but the Pharisees confess both. 23:6-8

The gospel preached by Paul was about the death, burial, and resurrection of Jesus. (1 Cor. 15:1-8) Seeking support from the Pharisees, Paul declared, "I am a Pharisee." The high priest was a Sadducee, and the Sadducees denied the resurrection of the dead. Paul identified himself with the Pharisees in their reverence

---

[72] John W. Wade, *Acts*, p. 239

for the Scriptures and their belief in the resurrection of the dead. Paul added that he was being judged because of the hope of the resurrection of the dead. The apostles of Christ were first arrested, because they "preached through Jesus the resurrection from the dead." (Acts 4:1-3) As Paul hoped, the Pharisees began to defend him.

There was a great uproar, and some of the teachers of the law who were Pharisees stood up and argued vigorously, "We find nothing wrong with this man," they said. "What if a spirit or an angel has spoken to him?" NIV **23:9**

The Sadducees and the Pharisees began shouting at each other as they debated about the resurrection and angels. The scribes who were Pharisees came to Paul's defense.

And when there arose a great dissension, the chief captain, fearing lest Paul should have been pulled in pieces by them, commanded the soldiers to go down, and to take him by force from among them, and bring him into the fortress. 23:10

The Sadducees wanting to kill Paul grabbed him pulling him in one direction, and the Pharisees wanting to save him pulled the opposite way. The Roman soldiers came again to Paul's rescue.

And the night following, the Lord stood by him and said, "Be of good cheer, Paul; for as you have testified of me in Jerusalem, so must you bear witness also at Rome." 23:11

The night after his appearance before the Sanhedrin, Paul must have been discouraged. For two consecutive days, his attempts to preach the gospel to his Jewish people had been interrupted by those who wanted to kill him. He was beaten, battered, and bruised both physically and emotionally. That very night, the Lord appeared to him to encourage him. Jesus told him to have courage, because he must go to Rome to witness to the gospel just as he had done in Jerusalem. Paul had accomplished more in Jerusalem than he realized. His explanation of his conversion in Acts 22:16 has helped many others to know what they must do to have their sins washed away by the blood of Jesus (Revelation 1:5). Paul's defense before the council was brief, but it may have led some to faith in Jesus. The Lord was also preparing Paul for the dangers that he was about to face, just as he did when he appeared to him earlier at Jerusalem (Acts 22:17-21) and at Corinth (Acts 18:9-13). But Jesus gave Paul the assurance that he would go to Rome. So whatever hardships were in the future, Paul's desire to preach the gospel in Rome would be fulfilled. (Romans 1:15-17)

And when it was day, certain of the Jews banded together and bound themselves under a curse, saying that they would neither eat nor drink till they had killed Paul. And there were more than forty who had made this conspiracy. 23:12-13

These men may have included Grecian Jews who had tried to kill him earlier (9:28-29), the Jews that accused him of bringing Gentiles into the temple (21:27-31) and the Sadducees that wanted to kill him the day before. These Jews mistakenly thought they were doing a service for God. (John 16:2) They believed that their plot against Paul would be carried out quickly.

They came to the chief priests and elders, and said, "We have bound ourselves under a great oath that we will eat nothing until we have killed Paul. Now you, therefore, together with the council, suggest to the commander that he be brought down to you tomorrow, as though you were going to make further

inquiries concerning him; and we are ready to kill him before he comes near." NKJV **23:14-15**

The chief priests and elders who heard this plot were probably Sadducees, because the Pharisees on the council had tried to protect Paul the day before. Wade writes, "The fact that these men were even willing to listen to this plot, which was both immoral and illegal, tells us something about the character of Jewish leadership at that point in history." [73] The Pharisees, who were not aware of the plot, would agree to a further examination of Paul. The commander would agree to the meeting because he still needed an accusation against Paul. The plan was to bring Paul from the fortress to the meeting place of the Sanhedrin, which was some distance away. Along the way these forty men would kill Paul. The Jewish leaders then would deny knowing anything about the plot.

So when Paul's sister's son heard of their ambush, he went and entered the barracks and told Paul. NKJV **23:16**

We are not told how Paul's nephew learned of the plot. But as soon as he knew it, he went to warn Paul. Paul could receive visitors, since he was being held in the fortress for his own safety. This is the only time any of Paul's family members are clearly mentioned.

Then Paul called one of the centurions to him, and said, "Bring this young man to the chief captain, for he has a certain thing to tell him." 23:17

The Greek word translated "young man" is used to describe men between twenty-four and forty years of age.[74] Paul's nephew was not a teenage boy.

---

[73] Wade, Ibid., p. 242
[74] J. H. Thayer, *Greek-English Lexicon of the New Testament,* p. 423

So, he took him and brought him to the chief captain, and said, "Paul the prisoner called to me and asked me to bring this young man to you, who has something to say to you." Then the chief captain took him by the hand, and went with him aside privately, and asked him, "What is that you have to tell me?" 23:18-19

The chief captain must have seen a worried look on the face of this young man that caused him to meet with him privately without delay.

And he said, "The Jews have agreed to ask you to bring Paul down tomorrow to the Council, as though they were going to inquire somewhat more thoroughly about him. So do not listen to them, for more than forty of them are lying in wait for him who have bound themselves under a curse not to eat or drink until they slay him; and now they are ready and waiting for the promise from you." NASB **23:20-21**

The chief captain then let the young man depart, and charged him, "See you tell no man that you have shown these things to me." 23:22

Their request would likely be made early the next day. The commander, Claudius Lysias, did not want the Sanhedrin to know that he knew about their plot. He said this for Paul's safety.

And he called to him two centurions, saying, "Make ready two hundred soldiers to go to Caesarea and seventy horsemen and two hundred spearmen at the third hour of the night; and provide them mounts that they may set Paul on and bring him safe to Felix the governor." 23:23-24

Again, the Romans would save Paul's life. He would be given a military escort to governor Felix at Caesarea for his protection. They would depart after dark, making it easier to keep the mission a secret. Horses were needed for Paul and his escorts.

He wrote a letter in the following manner: Claudius Lysias, To the most excellent governor Felix: Greetings. This man was seized by the Jews and was about to be killed by them. Coming with troops I rescued him, having learned that he was a Roman. And when I wanted to know the reason they accused him, I brought him before their council. I found out that he was accused concerning questions of their law, but had nothing charged against him deserving of death or chains. And when it was told me that the Jews lay in wait for the man, I sent him immediately to you, and also commanded his accusers to state before you the charges against him. Farewell. NKJV **23:25-30**

Claudius Lysias did rescue Paul, but not because he was a Roman. He learned of Paul's Roman citizenship after he had bound him to be scourged. (22:24-29)

Then the soldiers, as they were commanded, took Paul and brought him by night to Antipatris. The next day they left the horsemen to go on with him, and returned to the barracks. When they came to Caesarea and had delivered the letter to the governor, they also presented Paul to him. And when the governor had read it, he asked what province he was from. And when he understood that he was from Cilicia, he said, "I will hear you when your accusers also have come." And he commanded him to be kept in Herod's Praetorium. NKJV **23:31-35**

During the night the soldiers brought Paul to Antipatris, a town about 28 miles south of Caesarea. The next day, the soldiers returned to Jerusalem, and the seventy horsemen escorted Paul the rest of the way to Caesarea. Felix read the letter from Claudius Lysias; and after learning that Paul was from Cilicia, he kept Paul in Herod's Praetorium, not the common prison.

NOTES

Governor Felix Hears Paul
Acts 24

The Jews were disappointed when they learned that Paul had been taken to Caesarea to appear before Felix the governor. Their plot to kill Paul had failed. But the prophecy of Agabus in Acts 21:10-11 had come true. The Jews had caused Paul to be bound by the Romans. He would be a prisoner for more than two years at Caesarea (Acts 24:27) and more than two years at Rome (28:30).

And after five days, Ananias the high priest descended with the elders and with a certain orator named Tertullus, who informed the governor against Paul. 24:1

Five days after Paul had arrived at Caesarea, Ananias the high priest and the elders of the Sanhedrin came to Caesarea to bring charges against Paul before governor Felix. They came down from Jerusalem, which is 2,400 feet above sea level, to Caesarea which was on the coast. Tertullus, an eloquent lawyer, presented their case. He began his speech by praising governor Felix.

"Seeing that by you we enjoy great quietness, and that very worthy deeds are done to this nation by your providence, we accept it always, most noble Felix, with all thankfulness." 24:2-3

Roper states, "In truth, Felix put down several rebellions. However, he had done so with ruthlessness that enraged even moderate Jews." [75] And his corrupt nature was seen by his seeking a bribe for Paul's release. The Romans finally

---

[75] David L. Roper, *Truth for Today Commentary, Acts 15-28,* p, 369

acknowledged his wicked ways and removed him from being governor. (Acts 24:26, 27)

Tertullus began his accusation against Paul by saying, **"We found this man to be a troublemaker, stirring up riots among the Jews all over the world. He is a ringleader of the Nazarene sect and even tried to desecrate the temple; so we seized him. By examining him yourself you will be able to learn the truth about all these charges we are bringing against him." The Jews joined in the accusation, asserting that these things were true.** NIV **24:5**

First, Tertullus accused Paul of being a disturber of the peace causing riots among the Jews. He could point to disturbances among the Jews at Antioch of Pisidia, at Iconium, at Lystra, at Thessalonica and at Corinth. But Paul did not create these uproars; he was preaching peace between Jews and Gentiles. The Jews were the ones who were disturbing the peace.

The second charge brought against Paul was that he was **"a ringleader of the sect of the Nazarenes." 24:5** Jesus was called a Nazarene in contempt. (Matthew 2:23; John 1:46) Reese says, "Paul is being accused of founding a religion that is an offshoot of Judaism, and therefore unlawful in the Roman Empire ... not licensed by the state!" [76]

The third false accusation against Paul was that he **"even tried to desecrate the temple." 24:6** At first the Jews said that Paul **had** desecrated the temple (Acts 21:28); now they softened the charge by saying he tried to desecrate the temple. This would be harder to disprove. The Romans had given the Jews the right to execute anyone who defiled the temple.

---

[76] Gareth L. Reese, *New Testament History, Acts*, p. 839

Then Paul, after that the governor had beckoned to him to speak, answered, "Forasmuch as I know that you have been of many years a judge unto this nation, I do the more cheerfully answer for myself." 24:10

Paul did not use flattering words (1 Thess. 2:5), but was glad to make his defense before governor Felix, who had many years of experience in dealing with the Jews. Paul did not need an orator to present his case, because he knew that the Lord was with him. (Acts 23:11)

"You may understand that there are yet but twelve days since I went up to Jerusalem for to worship. And they neither found me in the temple disputing with any man, neither stirring up the people, neither in the synagogues, nor in the city. Neither can they prove the things whereof they now accuse me." 24:11-13

Paul said that he had just recently gone to Jerusalem to worship. He had gone quietly and peaceably. He did not argue with anyone or incite a riot in the temple or anywhere else in the city. Paul was not a troublemaker. The Jews could not prove that Paul had attempted to defile the temple with Gentiles.

"But this I confess to you, that after the way which they call heresy, so I worship the God of my fathers, believing all things which are written in the law and in the prophets. And I have hope toward God, which they themselves also allow, that there shall be a resurrection of the dead, both of the just and unjust. And herein I do exercise myself to have always a conscience void of offense toward God and toward man." 24:14-16

The Jews called the Way of Christ a heresy (a sect) of the Jewish religion, but they themselves were divided into the sect of the Sadducees and the sect of the Pharisees. The way Paul was worshiping the God of his fathers proved his faith in the law and prophets that predicted the coming of Christ. Paul emphasized in his preaching the great promise God made to the fathers, Abraham, Isaac and Jacob, saying, "In your seed shall all the nations of the earth be blessed." (Genesis 22:18; 26:4; 28:14; Acts 13:32-33) The "gospel" that all nations would be blessed was first preached to Abraham. (Galatians 3:8) The Jews were criticizing Paul for saying that Gentiles could enjoy the blessing of Abraham. Jesus Christ is the promised Seed by whom all the nations of the earth shall be blessed. (Galatians 3:16) Paul confessed that he served the same God that his ancestors had served for years. Paul was not starting a new religion; he was showing how Jesus Christ was fulfilling the oldest religion.

Under Roman law, Paul had every right to serve the God of his fathers. And Jesus proved that he was the fulfillment of the Jewish law and prophets when he was raised from the dead. Paul had hope in God because he was a witness that Jesus had been raised from the dead. He had seen him! Among the Sanhedrin elders at Paul's trial, there must have been some Pharisees, who believed in the resurrection of dead. In order to keep a united front, the Sadducees would not object to Paul's statement that his accusers also believed that there will be a resurrection of the dead, both of the just and unjust. Paul's speech and actions were governed by a good conscience toward God and man. He knew that he would be judged by God. Paul continued his defense:

"Now after many years I came to bring alms and offerings to my nation, in the midst of which some Jews from Asia found me purified in the temple, neither with mob nor with tumult. They ought to have been here

before you to object if they had anything against me." ^{NKJV} 24:17-19

The Jews from the province of Asia were the ones who stirred up the riot at the temple by shouting that Paul had brought Gentiles into the temple. Paul had not defiled the temple; he himself had been purified according to the Law. He was quietly worshiping God in the temple when Jews created the uproar by falsely accusing Paul. If the Jews had a case against Paul for defiling the temple, where were the witnesses? Who saw Paul with Gentiles in the temple? No one.

"These who are here should state what crime they found in me when I stood before the Sanhedrin—unless it was this one thing I shouted as I stood in their presence: 'It is concerning the resurrection of the dead that I am on trial today.' " ^{NIV} **24:20-21**

Paul called upon the elders of the Sanhedrin, who were present, to witness before Felix any misdeed on his part when he appeared before the council in Jerusalem. They might say that he caused a great uproar by saying, **"Of the hope and resurrection of the dead I am called in question."** (Acts 23:6-10) This was the reason Paul was being judged. Paul went from being a persecutor of Christ to being a preacher of Christ because he had seen the resurrected Christ. One of the greatest proofs of the resurrection of Christ is the conversion of Paul. And the resurrection of Christ is the foundation of our faith, as Paul had written in 1 Corinthians 15:13-17. If believing in the resurrection of the dead is a crime, then all the Pharisees on the council were also guilty. The Jews had no case against Paul.

But when Felix heard these things, having more accurate knowledge of the Way, he adjourned the proceedings and said, "When Lysias the commander comes down, I will make a decision on your case." So he commanded the centurion to keep Paul and let him have liberty, and told him not to forbid any of his friends to provide for or visit him. NKJV **24:22-23**

Cornelius the centurion and Philip the evangelist were among the Christians living in Caesarea. Hearing Paul gave Felix a better understanding of Christianity. Before making a decision, Felix wanted to visit with Lysias. In his letter, Lysias's account of Paul's arrest differed from that of the Jews. He believed that Paul did not deserve even chains, but the Jews were plotting to kill him.

Felix commanded the centurion to continue keeping Paul in protective custody in his headquarters. (Acts 23:35) Paul should have some freedom and be able to receive friends. Philip and other Christians would be able to visit Paul and provide for his needs. Luke was traveling with Paul when they came to Jerusalem (Acts 21:17); and he was with Paul when he left Caesarea two years later. (Acts 27:1) Luke probably ministered to Paul during his time in Caesarea, while gathering information that would be in his Gospel and in the book of Acts.

And after certain days, when Felix came with his wife Drusilla, who was Jewish, he sent for Paul and heard him concerning the faith in Christ. 24:24

Felix and his wife Drusilla wanted to hear Paul speak about the faith in Christ. Perhaps they were witnessing the faith, hope, love, joy, and peace in Christians. Although they had much of what this world has to offer; they didn't have what they were seeing in Christians. Felix had been a slave, but had been set free. Due to his connections with the Roman Emperor Claudius, Felix became governor of Judea. The Roman historian Tacitus said of Felix that "with every kind of cruelty and lust, he exercised the authority of a king with the temper of a slave." [77]

Drusilla was the daughter of the Herod that killed James the apostle. (12:1-2) She was Jewish through her great-grandmother, who was married to Herod the Great. Drusilla was known for her physical beauty. Felix seduced her from her husband when she was only sixteen, and she became his third wife. Roper says, "She was not yet twenty, but she was old in the ways of the world." [78] Felix and Drusilla needed to hear the gospel of Christ, God's power to save.

And as he reasoned of righteousness, temperance, and judgment to come, Felix trembled and answered, "Go your way for this time; when I have a convenient season, I will call for you." 24:25

Felix believed enough to tremble when he heard of his need for righteousness and self-control in view of the coming judgment of God. But he did not want to give up his sinful lifestyle at that time. He was waiting for a convenient time to change his ways. But that time never came. This is the mistake that many make today. They have enough faith to make them fearful and miserable, but not enough faith to be saved.

Meanwhile he also hoped that money would be given him by Paul, that he might release him. Therefore he sent for him more often and conversed with him. [NKJV] **24:26**

---

[77] Roper, Ibid., p. 381
[78] Roper, Ibid., p. 382

His desire for bribes was greater than his desire for righteousness before God. Each time he saw Paul and refused to repent, the more he hardened his heart.

But after two years Porcius Festus succeeded Felix; and Felix wanting to do the Jews a favor, left Paul bound. 24:27

Roper reports, "Felix was banished to Gaul (France) where he died. Drusilla and their son later perished in the eruption of Mount Vesuvius." [79]

---

[79] Roper, Ibid., p. 389

Paul Appeals to Caesar
Acts 25

Now when Festus was come into the province, after three days he went up from Caesarea to Jerusalem. Then the high priest and the chief of the Jews informed him against Paul, and besought him, and desired favor against him, that he would send for him to Jerusalem, laying wait in the way to kill him. 25:1-3

Three days after Festus became governor of Judea, he went up to Jerusalem from Caesarea. The Jewish leaders informed him of the charges they had against Paul and asked Festus to bring Paul to Jerusalem for a trial. Josephus informs us that Ananias was no longer high priest, but his successor, Ishmael, was just as ruthless and lawless. [80] They "desired favor" against Paul. For their co-operation in making peace between the Jews and the Romans, they wanted Festus first to hand Paul over to them for trial. They intended to ambush Paul on the way and kill him.

But Festus answered that Paul should be kept at Caesarea, and that he himself would depart shortly. "Let them therefore," he said, "who are able among you, go down with me and accuse this man, if there be any wickedness in him." 25:4-5

Festus appears to have been a fair-minded governor. Paul had the right to a trial in a Roman court. Festus was probably aware of Paul's Roman citizenship. Roman authority would determine the place. He suggested that those of influence and authority among the Jews go with him to Caesarea to make their accusation against Paul. God's providence was protecting Paul.

---

[80] Josephus, *Antiquities*, 20:8.8

And after he had spent not more than eight or ten days among them, he went down to Caesarea, and on the next day he took his seat on the tribunal and ordered Paul to be brought. ᴺᴬˢᴮ **25:6**

The KJV reads "And when he had tarried with them more than ten days," but the better text has "not more than eight or ten days." Luke knew that Festus did not spend more than ten days with the Jews in Jerusalem. On the day after his return to Caesarea with the leaders of the Jews, Festus took his place on the judgment seat that was called **the tribunal**, the symbol of Roman authority, and he ordered that Paul be brought before him.

After he had arrived, the Jews who had come down from Jerusalem stood around him, bringing many and serious charges against him which they could not prove; while Paul said in his own defense, "I have committed no offense either against the Law of the Jews or against the temple or against Caesar." ᴺᴬˢᴮ **25:7-8**

This time, the Jews did not have an orator to present their case in an orderly way; instead, they gathered around Paul and began making various charges against him. The scene was chaotic! Roper asks, "What could the Jews expect to accomplish by this hysterical outburst? Knowing that they would never indict Paul on their fallacious and fictitious charges, they evidently hoped to intimidate the new governor who was concerned about maintaining order in the land." [81]

But Festus, willing to do the Jews a pleasure, answered Paul, and said, "Will you go up to Jerusalem, and there be judged of these things before me?" 25:9

The Romans looked upon Palestine as a "powder keg." Festus wanted to make peace with the Jews, who were getting restless and rebellious. He needed the help of the

---

[81] David L. Roper, *Truth for Today Commentary, Acts 15-28*, p. 403

Jewish leaders. The case against Paul seemed to be more religious than criminal. Festus must not have known about the new plot to kill Paul.

Then Paul said, "I stand at Caesar's judgment seat, where I ought to be judged; to the Jews I have done no wrong, as you very well know. For if I am an offender or have committed anything worthy of death, I refuse not to die; but if there is none of these things whereof these accuse me, no man may deliver me unto them. I appeal to Caesar." 25:10-11

Paul knew that going to Jerusalem meant his certain death. He was willing to die if guilty, but Festus knew he had done nothing worthy of death (v. 25). Festus could not make him go to Jerusalem to be delivered into the hands of his accusers. As a Roman citizen Paul had the right to be judged by Caesar. Caesar was a title given to the Roman Emperors. Nero was the emperor at that time, and Paul appealed his case to him. Roper notes, "Knowing Nero's history of bloodshed, we may think it strange that Paul would desire to put his life in his hands. Keep in mind, however, that the first five years of Nero's reign were considered a "golden age" by the Romans. During this time, he was under the influence of Seneca, who was Gallio's brother." [82]

Then Festus, when he had conferred with the council, answered, "Have you appealed to Caesar? Unto Caesar you shall go." 25:12

Reese says, "The word "council" does not refer to the Sanhedrin *(sunedrin)*, but to the assembly of counsellors *(sumboulion)* who acted as advisors to the governor. Their chief function seems to have been to advise the governor on matters of Roman law, in this case, what an 'appeal to Caesar' entailed for him and for the defendant." [83] Festus

---

[82] David L. Roper, Ibid., p. 407
[83] Gareth L. Reese, *New Testament History, Acts*, p. 862

may have felt relief. He would not have to decide this case. As Wade wrote, "Festus saw that Paul's appeal gave the governor a perfect out. He knew Paul was innocent, and yet to release him would offend the Jews. However, by sending him on to Rome, he could be rid of the problem without angering the Jews." [84]

And after certain days King Agrippa and Bernice came to Caesarea to greet Festus. 25:13

Before Paul sailed for Rome, King Agrippa II and his sister Bernice came to Caesarea to welcome the new governor. At this time Agrippa was thirty-two years old, and Bernice was a year younger. He ruled over the territory just north of Galilee with his capital at Caesarea Philippi. Agrippa II was the last of the Herod kings. Being Jewish, he was also the legal guardian of the temple in Jerusalem and was given the right to select the high priest. The former governor, Felix, was married to his younger sister Drusilla. (24:24) Agrippa was living with his sister Bernice as his queen. This incestuous relationship was a scandal among both Jews and Gentiles.

And while they were spending several days there, Festus laid Paul's case before the king, saying, "There is a certain man left a prisoner by Felix; and when I was at Jerusalem, the chief priests and the elders of the Jews brought charges against him, asking for a sentence of condemnation upon him. And I answered them that it is not the custom of the Romans to hand over any man before the accused meets his accusers face to face, and has an opportunity to make his defense against the charges. And so after they had assembled here, I made no delay, but on the next day took my seat on the tribunal, and ordered the man to be brought. When the accusers stood up, they began bringing charges against him not of

---

[84] John W. Wade, *Acts*, p. 259

such crimes as I as I was expecting; but they simply had some points of disagreement with him about their own religion and about a certain dead man, Jesus, whom Paul asserted to be alive. And being at loss how to investigate such matters, I asked whether he was willing to go to Jerusalem and there stand trial on these matters." NASB 25:14-20**

Since King Agrippa was over the Jewish religion, Festus welcomed the opportunity to get acquainted with him; so they spent many days together. Perhaps, Agrippa could help him understand the case that the Jews had against Paul. Festus wanted Agrippa to know that he had acted promptly upon the Jews' complaint.

Festus expected the Jews to charge Paul with a crime such as murder or theft. But they accused Paul of saying that Jesus had been raised from the dead. Roper notes, "Festus conveniently failed to mention that his motivation for suggesting Paul be tried in **Jerusalem** was to please the Jews. The phrase **at loss** could be used to describe Festus' state of mind in general (see vv. 26, 27). He was hoping that the young king could give him insight." [85]

"But when Paul had appealed to be reserved unto the hearing of Augustus, I commanded him to be kept till I might send him to Caesar." 25:21

The Latin word "Augustus" was a title meaning "majestic dignity, worthy of reverence." The first Roman emperor Octavian was known as "Augustus." (See Luke 2:1) Other Roman emperors used Augustus as a title along with Caesar. The Roman emperor at that time was Caesar Augustus Nero.

Agrippa said to Festus, "I also would hear the man myself." "Tomorrow," he said, "you shall hear him." And so, on the next day when Agrippa had come together with

---

[85] Roper, Ibid., p. 415

Bernice, amid great pomp, and had entered the auditorium accompanied by the commanders and the prominent men of the city, at the command of Festus, Paul was brought in. ^{NASB} 25:22-23

The place of hearing was likely the Hall of Audience built by Herod the Great, the great-grandfather of King Agrippa and Bernice. Trumpets sounded as each special group was announced. The first to enter would be the prominent men of Caesarea, both Jews and Gentiles. The five commanders who were over the five cohorts stationed at Caesarea were next. Then Agrippa and Bernice entered dressed in their royal robes. And at last Festus was announced, and he came arrayed in the scarlet governor's robe. Festus then ordered that Paul be brought before this great assembly. And there Paul stood, dressed in his common clothes and prison chains. What a contrast! This was a fulfillment of a prophecy made by Jesus in Matthew 10:18, "You will be brought before governors and kings for My sake, as a testimony to them and to the Gentiles." ^{NKJV} Luke appears to be an eye-witness to this hearing.

Festus said, "King Agrippa and all you gentlemen here present with us, you behold this man about whom all the people of the Jews appealed to me, both at Jerusalem and here, loudly declaring that he ought not to live any longer. But I found that he had committed nothing worthy of death; and since he himself had appealed to the Emperor, I decided to send him. I have nothing definite about him to write to my lord. Therefore I have brought before you all and especially before you, King Agrippa, so that after the investigation has taken place. I may have something to write. For it seems absurd to me in sending a prisoner, not to indicate also the charges against him." ^{NASB} **25:24-27**

All the leaders of the Jews that had dealt with Festus in Jerusalem and Caesarea were demanding that Paul should be put to death. But the governor found that Paul had committed nothing worthy of death. Because Paul had appealed to Caesar, he had to send him to Rome. But Festus had nothing to write to Nero. He was asking for help. What charges could be brought against Paul?

Festus knew the charges against Paul by the Jews were concerning the Jewish religion. Because Agrippa had knowledge of the Jewish law, he was hoping that the king would be of help to him.

NOTES

King Agrippa Hears Paul
Acts 26

Agrippa said to Paul, "You are permitted to speak for yourself." Then Paul stretched forth the hand, and answered for himself. 26:1

King Agrippa II had requested to hear Paul. (25:22) Festus, the governor, was hoping the king could help him write the official charges against Paul after hearing him. This was not a trial; Paul was going to Rome to be tried by Caesar. So, Paul could speak freely and personally to the king, who was in charge of the hearing. Paul raised his hand as a greeting to his audience before he began to speak.

"I think myself happy, King Agrippa, because I shall answer for myself this day before you touching all the things where of I am accused of the Jews, especially because I know you to be an expert in all customs and questions which are among the Jews. Wherefore I beseech you to hear me patiently." 26:2-3

Paul was happy to present a reason for the hope he had in Jesus before the king. (1 Peter 3:15) Agrippa knew the law and the prophets and the customs of the Jews. He had been trained in the Jewish religion. Paul asked the young king to listen to him with patience, as he was seeking to lead him to have faith in the resurrected Christ.

"My manner of life from my youth, which was at the first among my own nation at Jerusalem, all the Jews know. They knew me from the beginning, if they would testify, that after the strictest sect of our religion I lived a Pharisee." 26:4-5

Paul respected the Jewish faith, even as a teenager in Jerusalem. Those who knew him could testify to his faith.

"And now I stand and am judged for the hope of the promise made by God to our fathers. Unto which promise our twelve tribes, instantly serving God, day and night, hope to come. For which hope's sake, King Agrippa, I am accused of the Jews. 26:6-7

What was "the promise" made by God to Abraham, Isaac and Jacob? *"In your seed all the nations of the earth shall be blessed."* (Genesis 22:18; 26:4; 28:14) This was the theme of Paul's preaching (Acts 13:23, 33, 38-48) and also of Peter's preaching (Acts 2:39; 3:25-26). The Jews were accusing Paul for saying that the Gentiles (the nations) could receive the blessings of the promise— the forgiveness of sins and the eternal inheritance in heaven. (Galatians 3:7, 26-29)

The hope of the twelve tribes of Israel was the coming of the Christ, who would bless all nations, but they misunderstood how the blessing would be fulfilled.

We hear some people today speaking of "the ten lost tribes." It is true that the tribes of the kingdom of Israel were scattered among the nations (the Gentiles) by the Assyrians, but they were not lost. (Amos 9:9-15) While ruling over all the nations to which Israel was scattered, Cyrus king of Persia decreed concerning God's people Israel, "Who is there among you of all his people? His God be with him, and let him go up to Jerusalem, which is in Judah and build the house of the LORD God of Israel." (Ezra 1:4) There was a gathering of all the tribes back to Jerusalem at that time. Anna, a prophetess in Jerusalem when Jesus was born, was of the tribe of Asher, one of the tribes that had been scattered by the Assyrians. (Luke 2:36) Jesus promised his apostles that they would judge "the twelve tribes of Israel." (Matthew 19:28) Hosea the prophet predicted that the children of Judah and Israel would be gathered under "one head." (Hosea 1:11)

Isaiah also predicted a second gathering of the remnant of God's people in Isaiah 11:11. This second return of the twelve tribes is in the gathering of Jews and Gentiles under one head, Jesus Christ. (Romans 9:24-27; Eph. 1:10, 20-22) F. F. Bruce commented, "The myth of the ten lost tribes plays no part in the biblical record." [86] The promise made to the fathers is fulfilled in Jesus Christ. (Galatians 3:26)

Paul had given the king and the governor the reason why the Jews wanted him dead: Paul was preaching that the promise made to their fathers was fulfilled in Jesus of Nazareth, who blesses both Jews and Gentiles. Paul then asked his audience this important question:

"Why should it be thought a thing incredible with you that God should raise the dead.?" 26:8

Jesus of Nazareth has been raised from the dead! This is the reason for Paul's preaching that Jesus had fulfilled the promise made to the Fathers. Why should it be hard to believe that God is able to raise the dead? Abraham believed that God could raise his son Isaac from the dead because God had promised, "In Isaac your seed shall be called." (Hebrews 11:17-19) He showed his faith by binding Isaac on an altar as God commanded, just before God made the great promise, "In your seed all the nations of the earth shall be blessed." (Genesis 22:9-18) Jesus, the promised seed, would die, but God would raise him from the dead. God had raised the dead in the days of the prophets. The son of the widow of Zarephath was raised from the dead by God's prophet Elijah. (1 Kings 17:8-24) Lazarus, who had been dead for four days, came from his tomb when Jesus called to him. The high priests and the council could not deny his resurrection, so they plotted to put Jesus to death. (John 11:39-53)

---

[86] David L. Roper, *Truth for Today Commentary, Acts 15-28*, p. 432

Paul now tells his audience why he went from persecuting the followers of Christ to preaching Christ as the fulfillment of prophecy.

"I truly thought with myself that I ought to do many things contrary to the name of Jesus of Nazareth. Which things I also did in Jerusalem; and many of the saints I shut up in prison, having received authority from the chief priests; and when they were put to death, I gave my voice against them. And I punished them often in every synagogue, and compelled them to blaspheme; and being exceedingly mad against them, I persecuted them even to foreign cities." 26:9-11

Paul had put innocent people in prison and was responsible for their deaths. He tried to force Christians to deny Christ. He became increasingly enraged. "Agrippa probably was surprised to learn that Paul had once persecuted Christians with as much zeal—or even more than—his own family, the Herods." [87] Paul was causing the young king to question: "How did this persecutor come to undergo so great a change?" [88]

"As I went to Damascus with authority and commission from the chief priests, at midday, O King, I saw in the way a light from heaven, above the brightness of the sun, shining round about me and them who journeyed with me." 26:12-13

In Acts 22:6, Paul says it was "about noon" when this great light appeared. It was brighter than the sun at the brightest time of day. All of those with Paul saw the bright light; they were witnesses.

---

[87] Roper, Ibid., p. 435
[88] J. W. McGarvey, *New Commentary on Acts of the Apostles,* p. 253

"And when we were all fallen to the earth, I heard a voice speaking to me and saying in the Hebrew tongue, 'Saul, Saul, why are you persecuting me? It is hard for you to kick against the goads.'" 26:14

The goad was a long sharp stick used to prod and guide animals. Stubborn animals would kick back only to their own hurt. Saul's persecution of the church caused it to grow and spread to other cities. This enraged him.

"And I said, 'Who are you, Lord?'"

In awe and fear, Saul wanted to know who was speaking to him from heaven. To his astonishment, his question was answered.

"I am Jesus whom you persecute. But arise and stand on your feet, for I have appeared to you for this purpose, to make you a minister and a witness both of these things which you have seen and of those things in which I will appear to you; delivering you from the people and from the Gentiles to whom I now send you to open their eyes and to turn them from darkness to light, and from the power of Satan to God, that they may receive the forgiveness of sins and inheritance among them who are sanctified by faith that is in me." 26:15-18

Jesus was speaking to him from his throne in heaven. He wanted Paul to be a witness to his being raised from the dead and to his ruling over the kingdom of God, predicted by the prophet Daniel. (Daniel 2:28-44) During his ministry, Jesus had said, "The time is fulfilled, and the kingdom of God is at hand." (Mark 1:15) Jesus promised Paul that he would reveal himself further to him, and he did. (Galatians 1:11-18) Why was Paul preaching to the Gentiles and promising them the blessings that God had promised? Jesus had made him his witness to the Gentiles to open their eyes, to turn them from darkness to light, from Satan to God; so they could receive the forgiveness of sins and an inheritance in heaven. Paul had seen the resurrected Jesus.

"O King Agrippa, I was not disobedient to the heavenly vision." 26:19

Could Paul be blamed for making such a dramatic change in his life? He had seen Jesus alive from the dead! And Jesus told him to preach to the Gentiles. All nations were to be blessed according to the promise. Paul quit persecuting Christians because he had seen the Jesus. One of the greatest proofs of the resurrection of Jesus is the conversion of Paul. And the resurrection of Jesus is the reason for believing he is the Christ. (1 Cor. 15:14-17)

Paul preached the gospel of Christ **"first to them of Damascus, and at Jerusalem, and throughout the region of Judea, and then to the Gentiles that they should repent and turn to God, and do works worthy of repentance. For these causes the Jews caught me in the temple and went about to kill me." 26:20-21**

Because Paul had been obedient to the heavenly vision, the Jews wanted to kill him.

"Having therefore obtained help from God, I continue unto this day, witnessing both to small and great, saying none other things than those which the prophets and Moses did say should come: that Christ should suffer, and that he should be the first that should rise from the dead, and should show light to the people and to the Gentiles." Acts 26:22-23

The gospel that Paul preached was not his own; he was being inspired by the Holy Spirit. Paul's witness was for all people. And it was confirmed by miraculous signs and by the writings of Moses and the prophets. Jesus was the first to be raised from the dead, not to die again. His resurrection gives us hope of life beyond the grave.

And as he thus spoke for himself, Festus said with a loud voice, "Paul, you are beside yourself, much learning makes you mad." 26:24

Like the Greeks in Athens, this Roman governor did not believe in the resurrection of the dead or life after death. He thought Paul was losing his mind. Festus felt compelled to speak up; he did not want any of his dignified guests to think for a moment that he believed such foolishness. Many today feel the same way toward those of us who believe in Jesus and the resurrection of the dead. To them such beliefs are not scientific, so they must be rejected by those who are enlightened.

Paul calmly said, **"I am not mad, most noble Festus; but speak forth the words of truth and soberness. For the king knows of these things, before whom I speak freely; for I am persuaded that none of these things are hidden from him, for this thing was not done in a corner." 24:25-26**

Paul had said he was "exceedingly mad" when he was persecuting the church (verse 11), but he is "not mad" for preaching the gospel of Christ. The teachings and miracles of Jesus were well known in Palestine, as were his crucifixion and his empty tomb. Then Paul said,

"King Agrippa, do you believe the prophets? I know you believe." 26:27

Paul knew by inspiration that King Agrippa believed the prophets. But he was not willing to repent. He said, **"Almost you persuade me to be a Christian." 26:28** The literal translation is: "In a little, you persuade me to make a Christian."[89] The name "Christian" had become a common way of speaking of a follower of Jesus.

---

[89] Alfred Marshall, *The Interlinear Greek-English New Testament*

And Paul said, "I would to God that not only you, but also all that hear me this day, were both almost and altogether such as I am except these bonds." 26:29

Paul wanted everyone to be a Christian like he was, except for his chains. The king then stood up along with the governor, and the meeting was over.

And when they were gone aside, they talked between themselves, saying, "This man does nothing worthy of death or bonds." Then Agrippa said to Festus, "This man might have been set at liberty, if he had not appealed to Caesar." 26:30-32

Festus must have written favorably of Paul in the official charges that were sent to Caesar. Paul was going to Rome! God had provided the way.

The Voyage to Rome
Acts 27

When it was determined that we should sail to Italy, they delivered Paul and certain prisoners to one named Julius, a centurion of Augustus' cohort. And entering into a ship of Adramyttium, we launched, meaning to sail by the coasts of Asia. Aristarchus, a Macedonian of Thessalonica, was with us. 27:1-2

When the time came for Paul's voyage to Italy, he and other prisoners were put in the custody of Julius, a centurion of the cohort of Augustus, which was one of the titles of the Roman Emperor. We are led to believe that this was the emperor's special cohort whose officers and men traveled throughout the empire on escort and courier duties.[90] **Luke** was accompanying Paul on this journey as indicated by the "we" statement. Being a physician, Luke may have been granted to come aboard to minister to Paul. **Aristarchus** of Thessalonica was another helper who was with Paul on this trip. He was one of the brethren who had journeyed with Paul to Jerusalem with contributions for the poor saints. (Acts 20:4) Earlier, he and Gaius were seized by the rioters in Ephesus, led by Demetrius the silversmith. (Acts 19:24-29) In Colossians 4:10 and Philemon 24, Aristarchus is mentioned as being with Paul in Rome. Friends of Paul had been allowed to serve him during his days as a prisoner in Caesarea. (Acts 24:23) They boarded a ship from Adramyttium, a city on the Aegean Sea near Troas. The ship sailed along the coast of Asia Minor on its way back to its home port.

---

[90] David L. Roper, *Truth for Today Commentary, Acts 15-28*, p. 452

And the next day we touched at Sidon. And Julius courteously entreated Paul, and gave him liberty to go to his friends to refresh himself. 27:3

The governor Festus must have reported to the centurion that Paul had appealed to Caesar, because the Jews were desiring his death over religious matters and that he and King Agrippa had agreed that Paul had committed no crime. Therefore, Julius treated Paul with respect and courtesy. Paul and Barnabas had passed through Phoenicia (including Sidon) on their way to the meeting at Jerusalem, "and they caused great joy to all the brethren." (Acts 15:3) Paul was allowed to visit with these friends in Sidon.

When we had put out to sea from there, we sailed under the shelter of Cyprus, because the winds were contrary. And when we had sailed over the sea which is off Cilicia and Pamphylia, we came to Myra, a city of Lycia. NKJV **27:4-5**

From Sidon they sailed north between the island of Cyprus and the mainland. A strong wind was blowing from the west, so Cyprus provided a shelter. Sailing along the coast, Paul's ship passed his home province of Cilicia and began heading westward, passing by the province of Pamphylia. Paul had begun his first missionary journey on the island of Cyprus, and John Mark had returned to Jerusalem from Pamphylia. Their ship landed at Myra in the province of Lycia.

And there the centurion found a ship of Alexandria sailing to Italy. 27:6

At Myra, Julius found a ship bound for Italy, so he put his soldiers and prisoners on board. The ship was carrying wheat (v. 38) from Egypt to Italy. This large ship from Alexandria, Egypt, was able to carry 276 persons (v. 37) in addition to its cargo.

When we had sailed slowly many days, and arrived with difficulty off Cnidus, the wind not permitting us to proceed, we sailed under the shelter of Crete off Salmone. Passing it with difficulty, we came to a place called Fair Havens, near the city of Lasea. ᴺᴷᴶⱽ **27:7-8**

An unfavorable wind made sailing westward difficult. From **Cnidus**, at the southwestern tip of the province of Asia, they had hoped to sail westward across the open sea to Greece and on to Sicily, but the wind did not permit it. Just before reaching Cnidus, they decided to use the northwest wind to sail south so they could sail **under Crete.** They rounded the Cape of **Salmone** on the eastern end of the island, and after sailing westward they arrived at a harbor called **Fair Havens**, which was halfway along the island and near the city of **Lasea.** They waited there several days hoping that the wind would change directions.

Now when much time was spent, and when sailing was now dangerous, because the fast was now already past, Paul admonished them, and said to them, "Sirs, I perceive that this voyage will be with hurt and much damage, not only of the cargo and ship, but also of our lives." 27:9-10

The Day of Atonement is "the fast" which came that year, AD 59, on October 5. [91] Between mid-September and mid-November was the dangerous time to sail. Paul was not speaking by inspiration but from experience, for he had suffered three shipwrecks already. (2 Cor. 11:25).

But the centurion paid more attention to the pilot and to the owner of the ship than to what Paul said. And because the harbor was not suitable to spend the winter in, the majority decided to put out to sea from there, on

---

[91] Roper, Ibid, p. 456, quotes Sir William Ramsey

the chance that somehow, they could reach Phoenix, a harbor of Crete. ᴱˢⱽ 27:11-12

The centurion trusted the advice of these experts, and the majority of those on board agreed that they should try to sail to Phoenix, which was a much better harbor on the western shores of the island.

Now when the south wind blew gently, supposing that they had obtained their purpose, they weighed anchor and sailed along Crete, close to the shore. But soon a tempestuous wind, called the northeastern, struck down from the land. ᴱˢⱽ 27:13-14

The favorable wind caused them to think they could reach Phoenix. At first, they thought they had made the right decision. But how quickly the winds may change! Suddenly a strong wind came from the northeast blowing their ship toward the southwest. They could not possibly arrive at Phoenix.

So when the ship was caught and could not head into the wind, we let her drive. And running under the shelter of an island called Clauda, we secured the skiff with difficulty. ᴺᴷᴶⱽ 27:15-16

Being driven by the wind, their ship passed south of the small island Clauda. While in the shelter of the island, they had a difficult time securing the swamped lifeboat which was towed behind the large ship. They had to pull it onto the deck and tie it down. Notice, Luke said "we" secured it. Luke helped.

When they had taken it on board, they used cables to undergird the ship; and fearing lest they should run aground on the Syrtis Sands, they struck sail and were so driven. ᴺᴷᴶⱽ 27:17

Roper says "These **cables** were ropes or chains placed around the hull and tightened with winches to hold the vessel together in the storm." [92] They feared that they might run aground upon the sandbars off the coasts of North Africa, called the **Syrtis Sands.** The ship was slowed down by lowering the main sail and yard arm, which also put less strain on the hull. The ESV gives the literal translation, **they lowered the gear**. If Luke meant they "lowered the sea anchor" (NIV), he would have used the Greek word for anchor as he does in verse 29. They were now at the mercy of the wind.

And we being exceedingly tossed by the tempest, the next day they lightened the ship; and the third day we cast with our own hands the tackling of the ship. 27:18-19

Those aboard the ship were being tossed about by the violent storm. To lighten the ship, **they began to jettison the cargo.** [NASB] This cargo was in addition to the wheat, which was thrown overboard later. (v. 38) The third day the tackling was thrown overboard, which included all things that were no longer useful because of the storm.

And when neither sun nor stars in many days appeared and no small tempest lay on us, all hope that we should be saved was then taken away. 27:20

It is depressing enough to go several days without sunshine. But in those days, before the invention of the compass, the sun and the stars were the only means of navigation. Besides the dark days and nights, the rain was pouring, the wind was blowing and they were being tossed about by the violent storm, and they did not know where they were. Could they be nearing a dangerous sandbar? They were gradually abandoning all hope. Even Luke was in hopeless

---

[92] Roper, Ibid., p. 459

despair. He wrote, "All hope that **we** should be saved was taken away."

But after long abstinence from food, then Paul stood in the midst of them and said, "Men, you should have listened to me, and not have sailed from Crete and incurred this disaster and loss." NKJV **27:21**

Wade writes, "This was not an attempt to say, 'I told you so.' Paul's purpose in recalling his earlier advice was so that they would believe what he was about to tell them now. His words would enhance his credibility as an expert. And what he was about to tell them was such good news that in their present hopeless condition, he needed all the credibility he could find." [93]

"And now I exhort you to be of good cheer; for there shall be no loss of any man's life among you, but of the ship. For there stood by me this night an angel of God, whose I am, and whom I serve, saying, 'Fear not, Paul, you must be brought before Caesar; and, lo, God has given you all them that sail with you.' Therefore, men, be of good cheer, for I believe God that it shall be even as it was told me. However, we must be cast upon a certain island." 27:22-26

This disaster at sea gave Paul an opportunity to testify of his faith. God whom Paul served had sent an angel that very night, promising there would be no loss of any man's life among them, but only the loss of the ship, because they would run aground on an island. Paul exhorted them to have courage because he believed God that it would be even as it was told him.

But when the fourteenth night was come, as we were driven up and down in Adria, about midnight the shipmen judged that they drew near to some country;

---

[93] John W. Wade, *Acts*, p. 274

and sounded, and found it twenty fathoms. And when they had gone a little further, they sounded again, and found it fifteen fathoms. Then fearing lest we should have fallen upon rocks, they cast four anchors out of the stern, and wished for day. 27:27-29**

It had been two weeks since they left Fair Havens. **Adria** refers to the central part of the Mediterranean Sea between Crete and Sicily. About midnight the shipmen believed they were nearing land; they probably heard the waves breaking on the shore. They began sounding for the depth of the water. The first sounding indicated **twenty fathoms**, or 120 feet. The second was **fifteen fathoms**, or 90 feet. They no doubt were glad that they were nearing land, but they were fearful they could not see rocks along the shore in the darkness of night. They protected the ship by dropping four anchors from the back of the ship to keep the ship headed in the right direction due to the wind blowing from stern to bow, and they waited for daybreak.

And as the shipmen were about to flee out of the ship, when they had let down the boat into the sea, under pretense as though they would have cast anchors out of the bow, Paul said to the centurion and to the soldiers, "Except these abide in the ship, you cannot be saved." 27:30-31

These fearful sailors tried to escape at night in the one lifeboat, pretending that they needed to anchor the ship from its bow. Paul recognized their deception, and warned Julius and the soldiers. The salvation of all aboard depended upon all remaining with Paul in the ship. "God has given you all them that sail **with you**." (v. 24) Everyone must stay in the ship! **Then the soldiers cut off the ropes of the boat. 27:32** Paul had the respect of the soldiers; they listened to his warning. The shipmen did not escape. Letting the boat drift away removed the temptation. They needed to trust in God and believe that it would be even as he had said. They all would be saved, but the ship would be loss. But in the meantime, they must stay in the ship. God's way is the only way to be saved!

And as day was about to dawn, Paul implored them all to take food, saying, "Today is the fourteenth day you have waited and continued without food, and have eaten nothing. Therefore, I urge you to take nourishment, for this is for your survival, since not a hair will fall from the head of any of you." And when he had said these things, he took bread and gave thanks to God in the presence of them all; and when he had broken it, he began to eat. Then they were all encouraged and also took food themselves. And in all we were two hundred and seventy-six persons on the ship. So when they had eaten enough, they lightened the ship, and threw out the wheat into the sea. NKJV **27:33-38**

Paul became the leader of those on board the ship. His courage and words of hope caused the soldiers and the sailors to respect him. They had been fasting for two weeks. Paul saw the need to strengthen their bodies, and he urged them to eat food. He saw the need to strengthen their spirits by saying, "not a hair shall fall from the head of any of you," reminding them of God's promise that they all would survive. Paul then showed his faith in God by taking bread and giving thanks to God in the presence of them all. When he began to eat, they all began to eat. The total number of persons on the ship was 276. After eating, they had the strength to cast their cargo of wheat into the sea to lighten the ship even more.

When it was day, they did not recognize the land; but they observed a bay with a beach, onto which they planned to drive the ship if possible. And they let go of the anchors and left them in the sea, meanwhile loosening

the rudder ropes; and they hoisted the mainsail to the wind and made for the shore. NKJV **27:39-40**

The land was the island of Melita, which today is now known as Malta. (28:1) To prepare for beaching, they cut loose the anchors and left them in the sea. Then they freed the rudders so they could guide the ship and raised the foresail that was also used to steer the ship.

And falling into a place where two seas met, they ran the ship aground and the forepart stuck fast, and the stern was broken with the violence of the waves. 27:41

Roper explains, "Two strong currents flowing from opposite directions had piled up sand and/or rocks under the water which the sailors could not see. These reefs, or strips of sand or rocks just below the surface, still exist at the traditional "St. Paul's Bay' in Malta." [94]

The soldiers planned to kill the prisoners to prevent any of them from swimming away and escaping. But the centurion wanted to spare Paul's life and kept them from carrying out their plan. He ordered those who could swim to jump overboard first and get to land. The rest were to get there on planks or on pieces of the ship. In this way everyone reached land safely. NIV **27:42-44**

Most of the prisoners were likely convicted criminals. If the prisoners escaped, the soldiers feared that they themselves would be put to death. Therefore, the soldiers asked Julius to give them permission to kill the prisoners. The centurion realized that the lives of everyone on board the ship had been spared because of Paul. To save Paul's life, he would not allow them to carry out their plan. The centurion may have ordered the soldiers to jump overboard and swim to shore first in order to collect the prisoners as they arrived. All 276 lives were saved. God keeps His promises.

---

[94] Roper, Ibid., p. 468

NOTES

Paul at Rome
Acts 28

And when they were escaped, then they knew that the island was called Melita. 28:1

Today, this island is called Malta. Paul's shipwreck appears to have been just two and a half miles northwest of Malta's capital city, Valletta. The island is about seventeen miles long and nine miles wide, located sixty miles south of Sicily.

The barbarous people showed us no little kindness; for they kindled a fire, and received us everyone, because of the present rain and because of the cold. 28:2

The people of the island were called **barbarous** because their common language was not Latin or Greek. Even today, they speak Maltese, a West Arabic dialect.[95] They were a highly civilized people as part of the Roman province of Sicily, having been settled by the Phoenicians by 800 BC. They showed great kindness to the cold, water-soaked survivors. They began building a fire.

And when Paul had gathered a bundle of sticks and laid them on the fire, there came a viper out of the heat and fastened on his hand. And when the barbarians saw the venomous beast hang on his hand, they said among themselves, "No doubt this man is a murderer, whom, though he has escaped the sea, yet vengeance does not allow to live." And he shook off the beast into the fire and felt no harm. However, they looked when he should have swollen or fallen down suddenly; but after they had looked a great while and saw no harm come to him, they changed their minds and said that he was a god. 28:3-6

---

[95] Francis H. Herrick, *The World Book Encyclopedia, Vol. 13*, p. 89

A fire was needed to warm and dry 276 survivors, so everyone gathered wood for the fire, including Paul, who was always willing to work with his hands. But as he threw a bundle of sticks on the fire, he was bitten by a poisonous snake. When Jesus gave the great commission to preach the gospel to the entire world, among the signs that would accompany the believers was they would not be hurt by serpents. (Mark 16:15-18) This miracle on Malta gave Paul an opportunity to tell the people about the true God. Roper says, "The deadly viper was probably one of Satan's last efforts to keep Paul from reaching Rome. God, however, used this incident for His own purposes." [96]

In the same quarters were possessions of the chief man of the island, whose name was Publius; who received us and lodged us three days courteously. 28:7

"In the providence of God, the spot where Paul and the rest were cast ashore was near the estate of the most important man on Malta." [97] Publius, the leading man of the island, graciously housed them for three days until more permanent arrangements could be made for the winter.

The father of Publius lay sick of a fever and of a bloody flux; to whom Paul entered in, and prayed, and laid his hands on him, and healed him. So, when this was done, others also which had diseases in the island came and were healed. They also honored us with many honors; and when we departed, they loaded us with such things as were necessary. 28:8-10

The people of Malta were a kind and hospitable people by nature, but when Paul healed the father of Publius and all their sick, it seems they could not do enough to show their gratitude. These miraculous signs also must have opened the door for Paul to preach the gospel of Christ to them.

---

[96] David L. Roper, *Truth for Today Commentary, Acts 15-28,* p. 483
[97] Roper, Ibid., p. 483

And after three months, we departed in a ship of Alexandria, which had wintered in the island, whose sign was Castor and Pollux. 28:11

The centurion had found another grain ship that was on its way to Rome. It had anchored in Malta for the winter because of the storm. Castor and Pollux were twin gods that the Romans regarded as the guardians of sailors. Roper says, "The passengers of the previous Alexandrian ship should have been impressed by this fact: The so-called gods of seafarers had done nothing for them. Rather, they owed their lives to the *true* God, the "one God, the Father, from whom are all things" (1 Cor. 8:6; see Acts 27:24)." [98] After the stormy season was over, they boarded the ship and sailed north to Sicily.

And landing at Syracuse, we stayed three days. From there we circled around and reached Rhegium. And after one day the south wind blew; and the next day we came to Puteoli, where we found brethren, and were invited to stay with them seven days. And so we went toward Rome. NKJV **28:12-14**

They stayed three days at Syracuse on Sicily's eastern coast. To reach Rhegium at the southwestern tip of Italy, they had to sail east and then north to make use of the wind. At Rhegium they waited a day for a strong south wind to take them through the Strait of Messina between Sicily and Italy, and then they sailed along Italy's western coast. A favorable south wind enabled them to reach Puteoli the next day. On the northern shore of the Bay of Naples, Puteoli was the place where the grain ships from Alexandria were unloaded to provide wheat for Rome. The brethren at Puteoli invited Paul and those with him to stay with them for a week. Julius the centurion probably agreed to a week's delay as a personal favor to Paul. Roper suggests, "Possibly he had been affected

---

[98] Roper, Ibid., p. 489

by the gospel and had become a Christian. Other soldiers became Christians, including some in the praetorian guard (Philippians 1:13)." [99]

Roper adds, "After a week in the port city, Paul and others in the official party started north on the Appian Way, the most famous of all Roman roads. What a sight that must have been: solemn Roman soldiers, sullen convicts, and smiling Christians!" [100] They continued their journey to Rome.

When the brethren heard of us, they came to meet us as far as Appii Forum, and Three Taverns. When Paul saw them, he thanked God and took courage. 28:15

Christians from Rome heard that Paul was on his way there, and they went out to meet him. One group met Paul at Appii Forum, some 43 miles south of Rome. Others met him at a town called Three Taverns, some 33 miles away. What a welcome! When Paul saw them, he was encouraged and thanked God. Appii Forum and The Three Taverns were resting stations on the Appian Way. Roper explains, "A tavern in the first century roughly corresponds to an inn or hotel today in that it included rooms in which to spend the night." [101]

When we came to Rome, the centurion delivered the prisoners to the captain of the guard; but Paul was permitted to dwell by himself with the soldier who guarded him. NKJV 28:16

Paul was not placed in prison but was permitted to live in his own rented quarters. (v. 30) Paul had friends in Rome, who likely provided the rent. (Romans 16:1-15) Paul was under house arrest, being chained to a soldier that guarded

---

[99] Roper, Ibid., p. 490
[100] Roper, Ibid., p. 491
[101] Roper, Ibid., p. 491

him. (v. 20) While being restricted, he could have visitors and was able to teach those who came to see him. (v. 30) Reese adds, "The presentation of his case in the letter from Festus, as well as a good word from Julius concerning Paul's conduct on the voyage to Rome, must have contributed to Paul's relatively mild bonds." [102]

After three days, Paul called the chief of the Jews together. 28:17

After securing a place to live and visiting with old friends for three days, Paul called for the leaders of the large Jewish community in Rome. Paul always spoke first to the Jews, so he invited them to come to him.

And when they were come together, he said to them, "Men and brethren, though I have committed nothing against the people or customs of our fathers, yet I was delivered prisoner from Jerusalem into the hands of the Romans, who, when they had examined me, would have let me go, because there was no cause of death in me. But when the Jews spoke against it, I was constrained to appeal to Caesar; not that I had anything of which to accuse my nation. For this cause therefore I have called for you, to see you, and to speak with you, because that for the hope of Israel I am bound with this chain." 28:17-20

Paul wanted the Jews in Rome to know he was innocent of the charges made against him in Jerusalem. After the Romans had examined him, they would have let him go. He had to appeal to Caesar because the Jews had objected to his being set free. However, he had no desire to bring charges against his nation. Paul wanted them to know why he was in Rome. He was a prisoner because of the hope of Israel. He desired to show them how Jesus had fulfilled the prophecies concerning the Christ and the kingdom of God.

---

[102] Gareth L. Reese, *New Testament History, Acts,* p. 935

And they said to him, "We neither received letters out of Judea concerning you, neither any of the brethren that came showed or spoke any harm of you. But we desire to hear of you what you think; for as concerning this sect, we know that everywhere it is spoken against." 27:21-22

The Sanhedrin had not sent them any official documents concerning Paul. They had not heard anything against Paul from Jews that had come to Rome from Judea. But they had heard of Christianity, which they called a "sect." They knew that everywhere it was spoken against. They desired to hear what Paul had to say.

When they had appointed him a day, there came many to him into his lodging to whom he expounded and testified the kingdom of God, persuading them concerning Jesus, both out of the law of Moses and out of the prophets, from morning till evening. 28:23

A large number of Jews came to spend the day with Paul, hearing him testify from the law and the prophets about the kingdom of God and showing that Jesus had fulfilled the prophecies. His was a message of hope.

And some believed the things which were spoken, and some believed not. 28:24

This response to the gospel message was common: some believed and some did not.

They disagreed among themselves and began to leave after Paul had made this final statement: "The Holy Spirit spoke the truth to your forefathers when he said through Isaiah the prophet:

" 'Go to this people and say,
   "You will be ever hearing but never
      understanding;
   you will be ever seeing but never perceiving."

> **For this people's heart has become calloused;**
> **they hardly hear with their ears,**
> **and they have closed their eyes.**
> **Otherwise they might see with their eyes,**
> **hear with their ears,**
> **understand with their hearts**
> **and turn, and I would heal them.'**
>
> **"Therefore I want you to know that God's salvation has been sent to the Gentiles, and they will listen!"** NIV **28:25-28**

Paul was quoting Isaiah 6:9-10, which described the Jews in the eighth century before Christ. People have not changed. Jesus applied these words to the Jews who rejected him. (Matt. 13:14) Hearts are hardened by one's own desires, causing them not to understand with their ears or perceive with their eyes. The Jews as a whole had closed their eyes to the truth. Therefore, the good news of salvation was sent to the Gentiles, who would receive it.

> **For two whole years Paul stayed there in his own rented house and welcomed all who came to see him. Boldly and without hindrance he preached the kingdom of God and taught about the Lord Jesus Christ.** NIV **28:30-31**

During this period of two years in Rome, Paul wrote letters to the Ephesians, the Philippians, the Colossians and Philemon. They are called "the prison epistles" of Paul because he was a prisoner in his own house. He was given the privilege to receive guests who heard him teach about the kingdom of God and the Lord Jesus Christ.

His theme was The King and His Kingdom.

NOTES

Bibliography

Ash, Anthony Lee, *The Gospel According to Luke, Part 1,*
The Living Word Commentary, Austin, Texas:
Sweet Publishing Company, 1972

Barclay, William, *The Gospel of Luke,*
Philadelphia, Pennsylvania: The Westminster Press, 1956

Bauer, Walter, **Arndt**, William, **& Genrich**, F. Wilber,
A Greek-English Lexicon of the New Testament,
Chicago, Illinois: The University of Chicago Press, 1974

Black, David Alan, *Learn to Read New Testament Greek Expanded Edition,* Nashville, Tennessee:
Broadman & Holman Publishers, 1994

Bruce, F. F., *The New Testament Documents,* Grand Rapids, Michigan: William B. Eerdmans Publishing Company, 1983

Herrick, Francis H., **Malta,** *The World Book Encyclopedia, Vol. 13*, Chicago, Illinois: Field Enterprises Educational Corporation, 1974

Josephus, Flavius, *Antiquities*, translated by William Whiston, Grand Rapids, Michigan: Kregel Publications, 1973

Josephus, Flavius, *Wars*, translated by William Whiston, Grand Rapids, Michigan: Kregel Publications, 1973

Lipscomb, David, *A Commentary on the Acts of the Apostles*, Nashville, Tennessee: Gospel Advocate Publishing Co., 1896

McGarvey, J. W., *A New Commentary on Acts of Apostles,* Lexington, Kentucky, 1892: reprinted by the Gospel Light Publishing Company, Delight, Arkansas

Perschbacher, Wesley J., ***The New Analytical Greek Lexicon,***
Peabody, Massachusetts: Hendrickson Publishers, 1990

Reese, Gareth, *New Testament History – Acts*,
Joplin, Missouri: College Press: 1976

Roper, David, ***Truth for Today Commentary, Acts 1 – 14***,
Searcy, Arkansas: Resource Publications, 2001

Roper, David, ***Truth for Today Commentary, Acts 15 – 28***,
Searcy, Arkansas: Resource Publications, 2001

Thayer, J. H., ***Greek-English Lexicon of the New Testament,***
Grand Rapids, Michigan: Zondervan Publishing House, 1970

Wade, John W., ***Acts,*** Eugene, Oregon:
Wipf and Stock Publishers, 2001
copyright by Standard Publishing 1987

Wilkinson, Bruce, **& Boa**, Kenneth, ***Talk Thru the Bible,***
Nashville, Tennessee: Thomas Nelson Publishers, 1983

www.ingramcontent.com/pod-product-compliance
Lightning Source LLC
Chambersburg PA
CBHW060822050426
42453CB00008B/541